American Indian
Love Lyrics

Also from Westphalia Press
westphaliapress.org

American Indian Love Lyrics and Other Verse from the Songs of North American Indians

Collected by Nellie Barnes
Forward by Mary Austin

WESTPHALIA PRESS
An Imprint of Policy Studies Organization

American Indian Love Lyrics and Other Verse from the
Songs of North American Indians
All Rights Reserved © 2017 by Policy Studies Organization

Westphalia Press
An imprint of Policy Studies Organization
1527 New Hampshire Ave., NW
Washington, D.C. 20036
info@ipsonet.org

ISBN-13: 978-1-63391-518-3
ISBN-10: 1-63391-518-2

Cover design by Jeffrey Barnes:
jbarnesbook.design

Daniel Gutierrez-Sandoval, Executive Director
PSO and Westphalia Press

Updated material and comments on this edition
can be found at the Westphalia Press website:
www.westphaliapress.org

American
Indian Love Lyrics

THE MACMILLAN COMPANY
NEW YORK · BOSTON · CHICAGO · DALLAS
ATLANTA · SAN FRANCISCO

MACMILLAN & CO., LIMITED
LONDON · BOMBAY · CALCUTTA
MELBOURNE

THE MACMILLAN CO. OF CANADA, LTD.
TORONTO

American Indian Love Lyrics *and* Other Verse

From the Songs of the
North American Indians

Selected by
Nellie Barnes

Foreword by
Mary Austin

THE MACMILLAN COMPANY
PUBLISHERS   NEW YORK
1925

PREFACE

ᏣHE influence of American Indian song-litera-ture has touched both the music and the literature of contemporary America. Those writers who use Indian themes are legion. Mary Austin has gone farthest, perhaps, among the writers of the day in relating her poetic work to the native rhythms of America.

These native rhythms pulsed through the songs of our Red Men for centuries before our Christian era. The very beautiful Aztec and the Inca poetry belong to the earlier and more highly developed civilizations. Since it is the purpose of this volume to treat of the more primitive forms of rhythm, it has seemed best to limit the illustrations to songs from tribes north of Mexico.

The late Mrs. Natalie Curtis Burlin's collection of songs in *The Indians' Book* makes that volume quite the most representative source book for the study of Indian lyrics. The original texts of unusual range in poetic patterns, the musical settings, the interlinear translations, and the accompanying narratives add a rich context to free translations of genuine literary merit.

Among other contributions to Indian song-

[5]

literature, the studies of Miss Alice Cunningham Fletcher, Mr. Carlos Troyer, and Doctor Washington Matthews hold a particular charm for the investigator.

Mrs. Austin's notable work, *The American Rhythm*, an analysis of the primitive poetic impulse, with illustrations from her own translations, came from the press after the writer's study of Indian poetic rhythms had been under way for some years. The conclusions for this volume have been limited, therefore, to those about poetic forms.

The writer is greatly indebted to Mrs. Austin for her generous interest in earlier work and especially for her helpful criticism of this study.

N. B.

Santa Fe,
July 29, 1925

FOREWORD

THE student of poetry in America enjoys an opportunity, such as has never been practicable for the European student, to come in contact with the source and mould of poetic form. For in Europe, the overlaying of all native activity by the sedulously cultivated Greek and Roman preferences, the deliberate turning of scholarly inquiry *from* what was self-sprung and indigenous *toward* what had been perfected in another environment and upon other roots, left the whole subject of the origin of form dangling in the atmosphere of theory and surmise. To this day the most that we know of the high forms of poesy in Europe is owed less to authentic tradition than to the scholastic rehumation of native remains in dance and ritual, of what was once, in the interest of the classic ideal, discarded and buried, or at the least, permitted to survive only among the unlettered folk.

Fortunately for our general understanding of poetic form, the Greeks had no such snobbish scruples as arose later throughout Europe against admitting the origin of their most majestic poetic medium in the communal dance around the tribal

altar. Here in the United States we are, by a
turn of fortune, undeserved and underappreciated,
able to watch the evolution of poetic form from
stages somewhat earlier than those recorded by
Aristotle, going on as an indigenous type of human
expression. We are face to face here with the
evolution of lyric form out of the stanzaic act,
ritualistically repeated; with the approach to the
ode, along the path struck out by primitive man
in the identification of himself with the sources
of high states of being.

We confront these things as unselfconscious
acts, rather than as fragmentary and over-anno-
tated poetic remains. We are able to refer them
directly to accompanying gestures, to generative
social occasions, and the environmental matrix.
And we have to guess or to theorize, where these
things are obligatory, only in reference to minds
whose movements are influenced by factors lying
open to intelligent apprehension.

To point this out, by way of introduction to the
first thoughtful attempt to put the material for
a valid conclusion as to the origin of poetic form,
in order for the unspecialized reader, is not to
subtract anything from the difficulty of the task,
nor to minimize the importance of the result.
So careless has American scholarship been of our
rich resources in this direction, that merely for
Miss Barnes to have realized their richness and

to have collected illustrative examples of them from the widely scattered and occasionally obscure sources, implies not only a general background of wide literary knowledge, but a fund of literary intelligence and much industry. It also implies a quality of restraint not infrequently lacking from such undertakings, in not attempting to bridge the gaps and supply the missing links by even the most plausible theory. Such restraint in view of the usual American demand for a complete tabloid statement, an assumption that does away with the necessity for further inquiry, is so much the more unusual that some of the credit for making this inquiry accessible surely devolves not only on the University in which it could take place, but upon the publisher who ventures to present it.

Merely by collecting from authentic sources, by discarding doubtful examples and by intelligent grouping of the best translations of Amerindian lyrics, according to their formative tendency, Miss Barnes has done more than perhaps she herself realizes, to uncover the influences at work on the primitive poetic impulse, to crystallize it into forms best suited to the expression of a progressively higher poetic content. To one who reads her simple statement of the relation of sacred numbers, fours and sixes and sevens, to what Miss Barnes calls the "thought rhythm"

as determining the form of primitive verse, and
reads it without other knowledge of Indians than
is included in these pages, it will scarcely appear
that the still profounder influence is the natural
environment, determining the force of climate,
landscape line, and food succession in the cultural
life of the particular tribe. But to one familiar
with environmental distinctions between Zuñi
and Iroquois and Omaha, there will be distinctive
pleasure in tracing relationships between verse
forms and the known formative features of the
given landscape. To such a reader there will
also appear intimate relations between the repeti-
tive pattern of formal elements, the range and
interdependence of dance movements, and of
decorative patterns of beadwork and textiles.
It would, in fact, be very little trouble to accompany each poem in this collection with an appro-
priate design either of gesture or decorative elements, drawn from the life of that tribe, in which
the distribution of formative elements would
make a pattern recognizably that of the poem. As
for example, in the Paiute *Lament of a Man for
His Son*, the gesture of the first movement would
be that inevitable to a man standing at the head
of his son's corpse, and striving beyond his grief
to descry his son's spirit walking the spirit road;
the gesture of the second movement, the reverent,
slightly swaying tread of friends bearing the body

on their shoulders over uneven ground; and of the last movement, the final tearing wrench of human affection. In the same manner, the *Iroquois Hymn* on the dissolution of the Great League, carries the gesture of up-flung arms, and the bowing of heads that dust may be cast upon them; while in the Navaho and Pueblo Rain Chants, there is the recurrent but always slightly variable motif of the landscape as the determinant of the verbal pattern, as you can see on any old Zuñi *tinaja*. It is the precision with which Miss Barnes makes these things appear to the initiate, without at the same time obscuring the more obvious conclusions for the average reader, which distinguishes what she has to say above all other writings on the subject. No one who reads her notes on Amerindian verse forms need feel the limitation of personal knowledge a hindrance to his æsthetic and intellectual enjoyment of the poems themselves.

I know of but one parallel to this achievement in the current descriptions of aboriginal culture in the United States. That is in George Bird Grinnell's account of Cheyenne games, in which, without saying as much, the relation of all games to man's aboriginal puzzlement about the world he lives in is convincingly brought out. Mr. Grinnell's account should be read in connection with Miss Barnes' work for the further light it throws on the origin of patterns, social, decorative, or literary, in living human impulses. In so far as any study does this, and especially as it does it in respect to areas of literary activity all too scantily familiar, it constitutes an indispensable service to American scholarship.

MARY AUSTIN.

CONTENTS

PART ONE

Indian Love Lyrics and Other Verse selected from
the songs of the North American Indians.

I SONGS OF LOVE AND FRIENDSHIP

II SONGS OF GRIEF

III SONGS OF NATURE (Secular)

IV SONGS OF RAIN

V SONGS OF THE SUN, MOON, AND STARS

VI SONGS OF DEITIES AND HOLY PLACES

VII SONGS OF INVOCATION FOR WELL BEING

PART TWO

[17]

AMERICAN INDIAN LOVE LYRICS

PART ONE

INDIAN LOVE LYRICS AND OTHER VERSE
SELECTED FROM THE SONGS OF THE
NORTH AMERICAN INDIANS

MY BARK CANOE (*Ojibwa*)

IN the still night, the long night through,
  I guide my bark canoe,
My love, to you.
While the stars shine, and falls the dew,
I seek my love in bark canoe—
I seek for you.
It is I, love, your lover true,
Who glides the stream in bark canoe.
It glides to you,
My love, to you.

HER SHADOW (*Ojibwa*)

OUT on the lake my canoe is gliding,
　Paddle dipping soft lest she should take alarm;
Ah, hey-ah hey-ah ho, hey-ah hey-ah ho, thus I go!
Somewhere along shore she is hiding,
She is shy to yield to love's alluring charm;
Ah, hey-ah hey-ah ho, hey-ah hey-ah, love will
　win, I know.
There is a shadow swiftly stealing!
Should it be her own, soon I will win the race;
Ah hey-ah hey-ah ho, hey-ah hey-ah ho, I think
　it is!
Will she but turn, herself revealing,
I will shout aloud when-e'er I see her face.
Ah! hey-ah hey-ah ho, hey-ah hey-ah ho,
There she is!

LOVER'S WOOING or BLANKET SONG (*Zuñi*)

I

O WHAT happiness!
How delightful,
When together we
'Neath one blanket walk.
We together
'Neath one blanket walk,
We together
'Neath one blanket walk,
We walk.
O! What happiness!
How delightful,
When together we
'Neath one blanket walk.
We together,
'Neath one blanket walk,
We together,
'Neath one blanket walk,
We walk.

II

Can it be that
My young maiden fair

Sits awaiting,
All alone tonight?
Is she waiting
For me only?
Is she waiting
For me only?

III

May I hope it is
My young maiden
Sitting all alone
And awaiting me;
Will she come then?
Will she walk with me?
'Neath one blanket
We together be,
We—we two, we two,
We two, we two—
Will she come?

PAPAGO LOVE SONG (*Papago*)

EARLY I rose
  In the blue morning;
My love was up before me,
It came running to me from the doorways of the
  Dawn.

On Papago Mountain
The dying quarry
Looked at me with my love's eyes.

LOVE SONG (*Dakota*)

𝔐ANY are the youths, many youths:
Thou alone art he who pleaseth me.
Over all I love thee.
Long shall be the years of parting!

THE BRIDE'S SONG (*Algonquin*)

THERE are many men in the world,
   But only one is dear to me.
He is good and brave and strong.
He swore to love none but me;
He has forgotten me.
It was an evil spirit that changed him,
But I will love none but him.

LONELY (*Ojibwa*)

FEAR not, he sayeth,
   Though far away,
Thy lover strayeth
At break of day.
"Go not, my sweetheart,"
Vainly I cry,
"To yon far island,"
Yearning I sigh.
Thither must I go,
Sadly I moan;
Heavy my woe,
Left here alone.

WAR SONG (*Dakota*)

FRIEND, whatever hardships threaten,
    If thou call me,
I'll befriend thee;
All enduring fearlessly,
I'll befriend thee.

ONONDAGA HYMN (*Iroquois*)

WOE! Woe!
    Hearken ye!
We are diminished!
Woe! Woe!
The cleared land has become a thicket.

Woe! Woe!
The cleared places are deserted.

Woe!
They are in their graves—
They who established it—
Woe!
The great League.
Yet they declared
It should endure—
The great League.
Woe!
Their work has grown old.
Woe!
Thus we are become miserable.

LAMENT OF A MAN FOR HIS SON
(*Paiute*)

Son, my son!
   I will go up to the mountain
And there I will light a fire
To the feet of my son's spirit,
And there will I lament him;
Saying,
O my son,
What is my life to me, now you are departed!

Son, my son,
In the deep earth
We softly laid thee
In a Chief's robe,
In a warrior's gear.
Surely there,
In the spirit land
Thy deeds attend thee!
Surely,
The corn comes to the ear again!
But I, here,
I am the stalk that the seed-gatherers
Descrying empty, afar, left standing.
Son, my son!
What is my life to me, now you are departed?

DEATH OF TALUTA (*Siouan*)

Ah, spirit, thy flight is mysterious!
   While the clouds are stirred by our wailing,
And our tears fall faster in sorrow—

While the cold sweat of night benumbs us,
Thou goest alone on thy journey—
In the midst of the shining star people!

Thou goest alone on thy journey—
Thy memory shall be our portion;
Until death we shall watch for the spirit.

WIND SONG (*Kiowa*)

O you warriors, you have loved ones
Longing for you, longing for you;
Rich are ye.
O you lovers, you have maidens
Longing for you; none have I.
Wherefore droop ye in silence, so downcast?
Cheer your hearts with song, ho!

BLUEBIRD SONG (*Pima*)

Hai-ya, *hai-ya,—hai-ya, hai-ya—*
  All my song is lost and gone.
Sad at heart is the bluebird,
All my song is lost and gone,
Woe is me, alas! alas!
All my song is lost and gone!

SONG OF THE UNHAPPY WIFE
(*Dakota*)

Sorely I am distressed;
  Sorely I am distressed;
Sorely I am distressed.
The earth alone continues long;
I speak as one not expecting to live,
Sorely I am distressed;
The earth alone continues long.

THE SONG OF UKIABI (*Cegiha*)

I AM walking to and fro!
I can find nothing which can heal my sorrow.

A LOVER'S LAMENT (*Tewa*)

My little breath, under the willows by the water-side we used to sit,
And there the yellow cottonwood bird came and sang.
That I remember and therefore I weep.
Under the growing corn we used to sit,
And there the little leaf bird came and sang.
That I remember and therefore I weep.
There on the meadow of yellow flowers we used to walk.
Oh, my little breath! Oh, my little heart!
There on the meadow of blue flowers we used to walk.
Alas! how long ago that we two walked in that pleasant way.
Then everything was happy, but, alas! how long ago.
There on the meadow of crimson flowers we used to walk.
Oh, my little breath, now I go there alone in sorrow.

MY HOME OVER THERE (*Tewa*)

My home over there, my home over there,
My home over there, now I remember it!
And when I see that mountain far away,
Why, then I weep.   Alas! what can I do?
What can I do?   Alas!   What can I do?
My home over there, now I remember it!

HUNTING–SONG (*Navaho*)

COMES the deer to my singing,
Comes the deer to my song,
Comes the deer to my singing.

He, the blackbird, he am I,
Bird beloved of the wild deer.
Comes the deer to my singing.

From the Mountain Black,
From the summit,
Down the trail, coming, coming now,
Comes the deer to my singing.

Through the blossoms,
Through the flowers, coming, coming now,
Comes the deer to my singing.

Through the flower dew-drops,
Coming, coming now,
Comes the deer to my singing.

Through the pollen, flower pollen,
Coming, coming now,
Comes the deer to my singing.

Starting with his left fore-foot,
Stamping, turns the frightened deer.
    Comes the deer to my singing.

Quarry mine, blessed am I
In the luck of the chase.
    Comes the deer to my singing.

    Comes the deer to my singing,
    Comes the deer to my song,
    Comes the deer to my singing.

A SONG OF THE DEER CEREMONY
(*San Carlos Apache*)

At the east,
Where the jet ridges of the earth lie. . . .

At the south,
Where the white shell ridges of the earth lie,
Where all kinds of fruit are ripe,
We two will meet.

From there where the coral ridges of the earth lie,
We two will meet.
Where the ripe fruits are fragrant,
We two will meet.

MOUNT KOONAK: A SONG OF ARSUT (*Eskimaun*)

I LOOK toward the south, to great Mount Koonak,
To great Mount Koonak, there to the south;
I watch the clouds that gather round him;
I contemplate their shining brightness;
They spread abroad upon great Koonak;
They climb up his seaward flanks;
See how they shift and change;
Watch them there to the south;
How one makes beautiful the other;
How they mount his southern slopes,
Hiding him from the stormy sea,
Each lending beauty to the other.

THE COYOTE AND THE LOCUST
(*Zuñi*)

Locust, locust, playing a flute,
Locust, locust, playing a flute!
Away up on the pine-tree bough,
Closely clinging,
Playing a flute,
Playing a flute!

KA-NI-GA SONG

THE poor little bee
     That lives in the tree,
The poor little bee
That lives in the tree
Has only one arrow
In his quiver.

CORN–GRINDING SONG II (*Laguna*)

BUTTERFLIES, butterflies,
Now fly away to the blossoms,
Fly, blue-wing,
Fly, yellow-wing,
Now fly away to the blossoms,
Fly, red-wing,
Fly white-wing,
Now fly away to the blossoms,
Butterflies, away!
Butterflies, butterflies,
Now fly away to the blossoms,
Butterflies, away!

SONG TO THE TREES AND STREAMS (*Pawnee*)

I

DARK against the sky, yonder distant line
Lies before us. Trees we see, long the line of trees,
Bending, swaying in the breeze.

II

Bright with flashing light yonder distant line
Runs before us, swiftly runs, swift the river runs,
Winding, flowing over the land.

III

Hark! O hark! A sound, yonder distant sound
Comes to greet us, singing comes, soft the river's song,
Rippling gently beneath the trees.

SONG TO THE MOUNTAINS
(*Pawnee*)

I

MOUNTAINS loom upon the path we take;
Yonder peak now rises sharp and clear;
Behold! It stands with its head uplifted,
Thither we go, since our way lies there.

II

Mountains loom upon the path we take;
Yonder peak now rises sharp and clear;
Behold! We climb, drawing near its summit;
Steeper grows the way and slow our steps.

III

Mountains loom upon the path we take;
Yonder peak that rises sharp and clear,
Behold us now on its head uplifted;
Planting there our feet, we stand secure.

IV

Mountains loom upon the path we take;
Yonder peak that rose so sharp and clear,
Behold us now on its head uplifted;
Resting there at last we sing our song.

RITUAL SONG (*Pawnee*)

I

O VER the prairie flits, in ever widening circles,
the shadow of a bird about me as I walk;
Upward turn my eyes, *Kawas* looks upon me,
    she turns with flapping wings, and far away
    she flies.

II

Round about a tree, in ever widening circles,
    an eagle flies, alertly watching over his nest;
Loudly whistles he, a challenge sending far;
    over the country wide it echoes, there
    defying foes.

WIND SONG (*Pima*)

FAR on the desert ridges
    Stands the cactus;
Lo, the blossoms swaying
To and fro, the blossoms swaying, swaying.

A SONG OF SPRING (*Chippewa*)

As my eyes search the prairie,
I feel the summer in the spring.

THE DARKNESS SONG FROM
THE INVITATION RITE   (*Iroquois*)

(The chief of the Invitation Rite requests all
the night folk of the forest to protect his people
on their journey to the morning.)

> WE wait in the darkness!
>   Come, all ye who listen,
> Help in our night journey:
> Now no sun is shining;
> Now no star is glowing;
> Come show us the pathway:
> The night is not friendly;
> She closes her eyelids;
> The moon has forgot us,
> We wait in the darkness!

THE INVITATION SONG

PART I (*The Song of the Whip-poor-will announced
by the flute*.)

I

So says the whip-poor-will,
    Follow me, follow me!
So says the chief to him,
Yes I will follow thee!

II

See the night darkening;
The shadows are hiding,
No light to follow for,
So says the waterfall,
So sings the river voice!

III

Someone is nearing me,
Soft he comes creeping here,
Two eyes glare close to me,
Lighting the forest path—
Hear how his breath blows by!

IV

Fol-low me, fol-low me,
So sings the whip-poor-will!
Yes, I am following,
So the chief answers him.

Part II (*The Wolf and his mate are announced.*)

I

Hark, the trees bending low,
Something is breaking them,
Not the strong north wind's hand,
Something stalks broad and swift.
Snuffing and panting loud!

II

Hark! How the tangles break!
Fearless the footfalls pass,
Strong trees stretch far apart,
Great horns dividing them.
(Whip-poor-will chorus)

Part III (*Buck and Doe with cries enter the room*)

I

How the cold shivers me!
No snow is falling now,
Where does the sun's fire hide?
Something comes roaring loud
Swift footed, warning me!

II

Its breath blinds the night eyes,
Like rainy vapor falls!
Now it walks close to me,
Warming and coaxing me,
Where the black forest frowns.
    (Whip-poor-will chorus)

Part IV (*The Bear and his mate have come.*)

I

How the wind travels now,
No one dares run with it.
Great trees bend low to it,
Rivers fight back to it,
Roaring and splashing it!

II

Hear its wings flapping strong
Far in the hidden skies!
Swift it flies northward high,
Whistling and calling loud,
Hunting its running prey!

(The Hawk and its mate are announced, and
all the rest of the forest folk. Finally, at dawn,
the eagle is announced by the flute.)

Part V   THE EAGLE SONG

I

Deep the dew water falls
No one comes close to me!
Where are you, whip-poor-will?
Why I am waiting now
Calling your voice again?

II

Screaming the night away,
With his great wing feathers
Swooping the darkness up;
I hear the Eagle bird
Pulling the blanket back
Off from the eastern sky.

III

How swift he flies bearing the sun to the morning.
See how he sits down in the trails of the eastern
    sky!
Whip-poor-will, Whip-poor-will, no more I follow
    thee!
When the night comes again, wilt thou say,
    "Follow me"?

THE PLANTING SONG (*Osage*)

I HAVE made a footprint, a sacred one.
I have made a footprint; through it the
blades push upward.
I have made a footprint; through it the blades
radiate.
I have made a footprint; over it the blades
float in the wind.
I have made a footprint; over it the ears lean
toward one another.
I have made a footprint; over it I pluck the ears.
I have made a footprint; over it I bend the
stalk to pluck the ears.
I have made a footprint; over it the blossoms
lie gray.
I have made a footprint; smoke arises from my
house.
I have made a footprint; there is cheer in my
house.
I have made a footprint; I live in the light of day.

SONG OF THE RAIN CHANT
(*Navaho*)

FAR as man can see,
  Comes the rain,
  Comes the rain with me.

From the Rain-Mount,
Rain-Mount far away,
  Comes the rain,
  Comes the rain with me.

'Mid the lightnings,
'Mid the lightning zigzag,
'Mid the lightning flashing,
  Comes the rain,
  Comes the rain with me.

'Mid the swallows,
'Mid the swallows blue
Chirping glad together,
  Comes the rain,
  Comes the rain with me.

Through the pollen,
Through the pollen blest,
All in pollen hidden

Comes the rain,
Comes the rain with me.

Far as man can see,
Comes the rain,
Comes the rain with me.

THE VOICE THAT BEAUTIFIES
THE LAND (*Navaho*)

I

THE voice that beautifies the land!
   The voice above,
The voice of the thunder,
Among the dark clouds
Again and again it sounds,
The voice that beautifies the land.

II

The voice that beautifies the land!
The voice below,
The voice of the grasshopper,
Among the flowers and grasses
Again and again it sounds,
The voice that beautifies the land.

CORN–GRINDING SONG (*Tesuque Pueblo*)

I

THIS way from the North
 Comes the cloud,
Very blue,
And inside the cloud is the blue corn.
  How beautiful the cloud
  Bringing corn of blue color!

II

This way from the West
Comes the cloud
Very yellow,
And inside the cloud is the yellow corn.
  How beautiful the cloud
  Bringing corn of yellow color!

III

This way from the South
Comes the cloud
Very red,
And inside the cloud is the red corn.
  How beautiful the cloud
  Bringing corn of red color!

IV

This way from the East
Comes the cloud,
Very white,
And inside the cloud is the white corn.
How beautiful the cloud
Bringing corn of white color!

How beautiful the clouds
From the North and the West
From the South and the East
Bringing corn of all colors!

SONG OF THE BLUE CORN DANCE
(*Zuñi*)

BEAUTIFUL, lo, the summer clouds,
Beautiful, lo, the summer clouds!
Blossoming clouds in the sky,
Like unto shimmering flowers,
Blossoming clouds in the sky,
Onward, lo, they come,
Hither, hither bound!

CORN-GRINDING SONG (*Zuñi*)

YONDER, yonder see the fair rainbow,
   See the rainbow brightly decked and painted!
Now the swallow bringeth glad news to your
   corn,
Singing, "Hitherward, hitherward, hitherward,
   rain,
         Hither come!"
Singing, "Hitherward, hitherward, hitherward,
   white cloud,
         Hither come!"
Now we hear the corn-plants murmur,
         "We are growing everywhere!"
         Hi, yai, the world, how fair!

CORN DANCE SONG (*Zuñi*)

WHO, ah ye know who—
　　Who, ah ye know who—
Who was't that made a picture the first?
It was the bright Rainbow Youth,
　　　　Rainbow Youth—
Ay, behold it was even thus—
　　　　Clouds came,
　　　　And rain came
　　　　Close following—
Rainbow then colored all!

KOROSTA KATZINA SONG (*Hopi*)

I

YELLOW butterflies
  Over the blossoming virgin corn,
With pollen-painted faces
Chase one another in brilliant throng.

II

Blue butterflies
Over the blossoming virgin beans,
  With pollen-painted faces
Chase one another in brilliant streams.

III

Over the blossoming corn,
Over the virgin corn
Wild bees hum;
Over the blossoming corn,
Over the virgin beans
Wild bees hum.

IV

Over your field of growing corn
All day shall hang the thunder-cloud;
Over your field of growing corn
All day shall come the rushing rain.

ANGA KATZINA SONG (*Hopi*)

RAIN all over the cornfields,
    Pretty butterfly-maidens
Chasing one another when the rain is done,
    Hither, thither, so.
How they frolic 'mid the corn,
    Laughing, laughing, thus:
        A-ha, ha-ha,
        O-ah, e-lo!
How they frolic 'mid the corn,
    Singing, singing, thus:
        O-o, o-ho,
        O-he, e-lo!

HE–HEA KATZINA SONG (*Hopi*)

CORN-BLOSSOM maidens
Here in the fields,
Patches of beans in flower,
Fields all abloom,
Water shining after rain,
Blue clouds looming above.

Now behold!
Through bright clusters of flowers
Yellow butterflies
Are chasing at play,
And through the blossoming beans
Blue butterflies
Are chasing at play.

WUWUCHIM–CHANT (*Hopi*)

THUS we, thus we,
  The night along,
With happy hearts
Wish well one another.

In the chief's kiva
They, the fathers,
They and Muyingwa
Plant the double ear—
Plant the perfect double corn-ear.
So the fields shall shine
With tassels white of perfect corn-ears.

Hither to them, hither come,
Rain that stands and cloud that rushes!

A RAIN SONG OF THE SNAKE
SOCIETY — I (*Sia*)

PRIESTS of *tinia*,
  Let the white floating clouds,
The clouds like the plains,
The lightning, thunder, rainbow, and cloud
    peoples water the earth.
Let the people of the white floating clouds,
The people of the‧ clouds like the plains,
The lightning, thunder, rainbow, and cloud
    peoples
Come and work for us and water the earth.

A RAIN SONG OF THE SNAKE
SOCIETY—II (*Sia*)

CLOUD priest who ascends through the heart
    of the spruce of the north,
Cloud priest who ascends through the heart of the
    pine of the west,
Cloud priest who ascends through the heart of the
    oak of the south,
Cloud priest who ascends through the heart of the
    aspen of the east,
Cloud priest who ascends through the heart of the
    cedar of the zenith,
Cloud priest who ascends through the heart of the
    oak of the nadir,
Send your people to work for us
That the water of the six great springs may
    quicken the earth,
That she may give to us the fruits of her being.

CORN SONG (*Pima*)

I

H*i-ilo-o ya-a-a!* He who sees everything
    Sees the two stalks of corn standing;
He's my younger brother. *Hi-ilo-o- ya-a-a!*
    He who sees everything, sees the two
        squashes;
He's my younger brother. *Hi-ilo-o ya-a-a!*
    On the summit of *Ta-atûkam* sees the corn
        standing;
He's my younger brother. *Hi-ilo- ya-a-a!*
    On the summit of *Ta-atûkam* sees the squash
        standing;
He's my younger brother. *Hi-ilo-o woiha!*

II

Hi-ilo-o ya-a-a! Over *Ta-atûkam*
    Rise the clouds with their loud thundering.
Hi-ilo-o ya-a-a! Over *Ta-atûkam*
    Rise the clouds with their loud raining.
Hi-ilo-o ya-a-a! The Bluebird is holding
    In his talons the clouds that are thundering.
Hi-ilo-o ya-a-a! Yellowbird is holding
    In his talons the clouds that are raining.

III

Hi-ilo-o ya-a-a! See Elder Brother
    Breathe out the winds that over *Ta-atûkam*
Drive the clouds with their loud thundering.
    Hi-ilo-o ya-a-a! See Elder Brother
Breathe out the winds that over *Ta-atûkam*
    The welcome storm clouds are suspending.
Hi-ilo-o ya-a-a! In the great rain clouds
    Let me sing my song of rejoicing.

RAIN SONGS (*Pima*)

I

Hi-*ihiya naiho-o!* Let us begin our song,
  Let us begin, rejoicing. *Hitciya yahina-a.*
Let us begin our song, let us begin, rejoicing,
  Singing of the large corn. *Hitciya yahina-a.*
Singing of the small corn. *Hitciya yahina-a.*

II

Hi-ihiya naiho-o! The darkness of evening
  Falls as we sing before the sacred âmĭna.
About us on all sides corn tassels are waving.
  Hitciya yahina! The white light of day dawn
Yet finds us singing, while corn tassels are waving.
  Hitciya yahina-a! The darkness of evening
Falls as we sing before the sacred âmĭna.
  About us on all sides corn tassels are waving.
Hitciya yahina! The white light of day dawn
  Yet finds us singing, while the squash leaves
    are waving.

III

Hi-iya naiho-o! The earth is rumbling
  From the beating of our basket drums.

The earth is rumbling from the beating
　　　Of our basket drums, everywhere humming.
　　　　　Hitciya yahina-a.
Earth is rumbling, everywhere raining,
　　　　　Hitciya yahina-a.

IV

Hi-ihiya naiho-o! Pluck out the feathers
　　　From the wing of the Eagle and turn them
Toward the east where lie the large clouds.
　　　Hitciya yahina-a! Pluck out the soft down
From the breast of the Eagle and turn it
　　　Toward the west where sail the small clouds.
Hitciya yahina! Beneath the abode
　　　Of the rain gods it is thundering;
Large corn is there. *Hitciya yahina!*
　　　Beneath the abode of the rain gods
It is raining; small corn is there.
　　　　　Hitciya yahina.

A METATE SONG

Is it not beautiful?
Is it not, truly!

Is it not beautiful?
Is it not, truly!

Is it not beautiful?
Is it not, truly!

Is it not beautiful?
Is it not, truly!

Is it not beautiful?
Is it not, truly!

On every side They are,
The Trues, the rain-commanders;
Do you not hear their drum?
Because of that you will see
This year the vapor floating;
Because of that you will see
This year the drizzling rain.

Is it not beautiful?
Is it not truly!

In all the fields the corn upspringing,
Like the young pine it comes up;
Like the green aspen;
In all the fields the corn upspringing,
Tall like the tail of the thrush!
Tall like the road-runner's tail,
In all the fields the corn upspringing!

(Refrain of three lines of vocables.)

FLUTE SONG (*Hopi*)

I

HAIL, fathers, hail!
    Chieftain of the Gray Flute, hail!
At the four world-points
Ye call, ye summon clouds.
From the four world-points upstarting,
Shall the rain hither come.

II

Hither thunder, rain-thunder here,
Hither the rain-thunder will come;
Hither rain, moving-rain—
Onward now, over all the fields,
Moving-rain.
And the wet earth, amid the corn,
Everywhere, far and near,
It will shine—water-shine.

THE SUNRISE CALL (*Zuñi*)

I

ISE! arise! arise!
Rise! arise, arise!
Wake ye! arise, life is greeting thee.
Wake ye, arise, ever watchful be.
Mother Life-god, she is calling thee!
Mother Life-god, she is calling thee!
Mother Life-god, she is greeting thee.
All arise, arise, arise!
Rise! arise, arise!

II

Mighty Sun-god! give thy light to us,
Let it guide us, let it aid us.
See it rise! See it rise!
How the heart glows, how the soul delights,
In the music of the sunlight.
Watch it rise! Watch it rise!
Wake ye, arise, life is greeting thee.
Wake ye, arise, ever watchful be.
Mother Life-god, she is calling thee!
Mother Life-god she is greeting thee.
All arise, arise, arise!
Rise! arise, arise!

HYMN TO THE SUN (*Zuñi*)

I

EARLY in the morning,
    We waken, we waken.
When mother Sun-god rises,
We welcome her with joy.
She greets us with a radiant face,
She meets us with a warm embrace,
So sweetly, so sweetly.
Merrily we sing and dance;
In happy spirit we advance;
Merrily we sing and dance;
In happy spirit we advance.
We are children of the sun,
Arm in arm together run,
Round a ring we steady move:
Our hearts will faithful prove,
As the sun comes near to us,
Near to us, near to us.
Listen! just listen!

II

What a wondrous shower of sounds,
Countless beats in rapid rounds,
Ever changing ever new,

Constant strains of high and low.
They are messengers of love,
Spirit voices from above,
Bringing light and life and joy
Telling us of bliss on high,
Bliss on high! Bliss on high!
Listen! just listen!

III

Whence come all these distant sounds?
Echoes, where the light abounds:
Crystal streams in murmurs faint,
Bursting forth without restraint.
They are golden grains of thought,
Silent whispers faintly caught,
Filling us with joy content,
Pathways of our souls' ascent,
Souls' ascent, souls' ascent.
Listen! just listen!

IV

Glory to the sunlight rays,
Glory to the Sun-god's ways,
Sunlight rays, Sun-god's ways.
They command us: to endure,
To be silent, chaste and pure,
To be faithful, true and brave,
To the laws our fathers gave.

O harken to the Sun-god's voice
Beckoning your soul to rise:
In radiant light, the source of song,
The origin of thought has sprung:
As light and song in one unite,
Let us forever seek the light,
We seek the light, we seek the light.
Listen! just listen!

SUNSET SONG (*Zuñi*)

GOODNIGHT to thee, Fair Goddess,
  We thank thee for thy blessing.
Goodnight to thee, Fair Goddess,
We thank thee for this day.
In glory we behold thee
At early dawn again.
We thank thee for thy blessing,
To be with us this day.
This day,
We thank thee for this day.

INVOCATION TO THE SUN-GOD
(*Zuñi*)

GRANT, O Sun-god, thy protection!
  Guard this helpless infant sleeping.
Grant, O Sun-god, thy protection!
Guard this helpless infant sleeping,
Resting peaceful, resting peaceful.
Starry guardians forever joyful,
Faithful Moon-god forever watchful.
Grant, O Sun-god, thy protection!
Guard this helpless infant sleeping.
Spirit living, Spirit resting,
Guard us, lead us, aid us, love us.
Sun-god forever, Spirit living, Spirit resting,
Guard us, lead us, aid us, love us,
Sun-god forever.

A SONG OF GOTAL LIII (*Mescalero Apache*)

T HE black turkey-gobbler, under the East, the middle of his tail; toward us it is about to dawn.

The black turkey-gobbler, the tips of his beautiful tail; above us the dawn whitens.

The black turkey-gobbler, the tips of his beautiful tail; above us the dawn becomes yellow.

The sunbeams stream forward, dawn boys, with shimmering shoes of yellow;

On top of the sunbeams that stream toward us they are dancing.

At the East the rainbow moves forward, dawn maidens, with shimmering shoes and shirts of yellow dance over us.

Beautifully over us it is dawning.

Above us among the mountains the herbs are becoming green;

Above us on the tops of the mountains the herbs are becoming yellow.

Above us among the mountains, with shoes of yellow I go around the fruits and herbs that shimmer.

Above us among the mountains, the shimmering fruits with shoes and shirts of yellow are bent toward him.

On the beautiful mountains above it is daylight.

FIRST DAYLIGHT SONG (*Navaho*)

I

THE curtain of daybreak is hanging,
The Daylight Boy (it is hanging),
From the land of day it is hanging;
Before him, as it dawns, it is hanging.
Behind him, as it dawns, it is hanging.
Before him, in beauty, it is hanging;
Behind him, in beauty, it is hanging;
From his voice, in beauty, it is hanging.

II

The Daylight Girl (it is hanging),
From the land of yellow light, it is hanging;
Before her, as it dawns, it is hanging;
Behind her, as it dawns, it is hanging.
Before her, in beauty, it is hanging;
Behind her, in beauty, it is hanging;
From her voice, in beauty, it is hanging.

SONG OF THE DAWN BOY (*Navaho*)

WHERE my kindred dwell, there I wander.
Child of the White Corn am I, there I
wander.
The Red Rock House, there I wander.
Where dark *kethawns* are at the doorway, there
I wander.
At the *yuni*, the striped cotton hangs with pol-
len. There I wander,
Going around with it. There I wander.
Taking another, I depart with it. With it I
wander.
In the house of long life, there I wander.
In the house of happiness, there I wander.
Beauty before me, with it I wander.
Beauty behind me, with it I wander,
Beauty below me, with it I wander,
Beauty above me, with it I wander.
Beauty all around me, with it I wander,
In old age traveling, with it I wander.
On the beautiful trail I am, with it I wander.

THE MORNING STAR AND THE
NEW BORN DAWN (*Pawnee*)

I

O MORNING Star, for thee we watch!
  Dimly comes thy light from distant skies;
We see thee, then lost art thou,
Morning Star, thou bringest life to us.

II

O Morning Star, thy form we see!
Clad in shining garments dost thou come,
Thy plume touched with rosy light.
Morning Star, thou now art vanishing.

III

O youthful Dawn, for thee we watch!
Dimly comes thy light from distant skies;
We see thee, then lost art thou.
Youthful Dawn, thou bringest life to us.

IV

O youthful Dawn, we see thee come!
Bright grows thy glowing light
As near, nearer thou dost come.
Youthful Dawn, thou now art vanishing.

DAYLIGHT (*Pawnee*)

I

DAY is here! Day is here, is here!
　　Arise, my son, lift thine eyes,
Day is here! Day is here, is here!
Day is here! Day is here, is here!
Look up, my son, and see the day.
Day is here! Day is here, is here!

II

Lo, the deer! Lo, the deer, the deer
Comes from her covert of the night!
Day is here! Day is here, is here!
Lo, the deer! Lo, the deer, the deer!
All creatures wake and see the light.
Day is here! Day is here, is here!
Day is here! Day is here, is here!

THE BIRTH OF DAWN (*Pawnee*)

I

A WAKE, O mother, from sleep!
Awake! the night is far spent;
The signs of dawn are now seen
In east, whence cometh new life.

II

The mother wakens from sleep;
She wakes, for night is far spent;
The signs of dawn are now seen
In east, whence cometh new life.

III

Awake, O *Kawas*, from sleep!
Awake! The night is far spent;
The signs of dawn are now seen
In east, whence cometh new life.

IV

Now *Kawas* wakens from sleep,
Awakens for night is far spent;
The signs of dawn are now seen
In east, whence cometh new life.

[89]

V

Then *Kawas* stands and speaks forth:
"A child from Night is now born;
Tirá wa, father on high,
On Darkness moving, brings Dawn."

VI

I understand now, I know
A child from Night has been born;
Tirá wa, father on high,
On Darkness moving, brings Dawn.

VII

O Son, awaken from sleep
Awake! the night is far spent;
The signs of dawn are now seen
In east, whence cometh new life.

VIII

The Son awakens from sleep;
He wakes, for night is far spent;
The signs of dawn are now seen
In east, whence cometh new life.

SONG TO THE PLEIADES (*Pawnee*)

Look as they rise, rise
Over the line where sky meets the earth;
Pleiades!
Lo! They ascending, come to guide us,
Leading us safely, keeping us one;
Pleiades,
Teach us to be, like you, united.

THE SONG OF THE STARS
(Algonquin)

WE are the stars which sing,
  We sing with our light;
We are the birds of fire,
We fly over the sky.
Our light is a voice;
We make a road for spirits,
For the spirits to pass over.
Among us are three hunters
Who chase a bear;
There never was a time
When they were not hunting.
We look down on the mountains.
This is the Song of the Stars.

THE STARS DEHN-DEK AND
MAH-OH-RAH (*Wyandot*)

DEHN-DEK (*to Oh-tsch-eh-stah, the mother*):
  She arises from the ground!
In a far land Mah-oh-rah walks before us!
She comes to the great city and stands
    before its gates!
Our Grandmother looks upon her! She who
    fell down from heaven, . . . lies upon
    her couch and beholds Mah-oh-rah.
She goes to the Land of Little People; she
    goes through the old city in which our
    fathers were saved.
Get thee down in haste and bring her again
    to her own people.
(*Journeys forth to the city of Our Grandmother.*)

(*Enters the royal palace in the sacred city.*)

Dehn-dek (*to Our Grandmother*):
  Give again into my arms the daughter gone
    to the Land of the Little People!
She stood here in this hour, but is gone on
    the lonely way to that land.
Your children mourn for her; they cut
    themselves for grief!
Let her return with me to our own land.

Our Grandmother:
    Mah-oh-rah stood indeed before me!
    She was pale and faint from the journey!
    The Hooh-kehs drew her back in their
        power!
    She went out from my presence to return to
        her own people.
    Two torches she bore aloft to make clear
        the way.

(*Dehn-dek goes out in pursuit of his daughter.*)

Our Grandmother (*watching the pursuit*):
    They go into the sky!
    From that land are we cast down forever!
    And another land is made for us.
    Let them be made stars.
    Now shall they be made stars to shine
        forever there.
    And their journey shall never cease!

SONG OF THE MASKED DANC-ERS (*Apache*)

T HE day broke with slender rain.
  The place which is called "lightning's water
    stands,"
The place which is called "where the dawn
    strikes,"
Four places where it is called "it dawns with
    life,"
I landed there.
I went among the sky youths.
One came to me with long life.
When he talked over my body with the longest
    life,
The voice of the thunder spoke well four times,
He spoke four times to me with life.
Holy sky youth spoke to me four times.
When he talked to me my breath became.

A SONG OF THE MASKED DANC–
ERS III (*Apache*)

THE living sky black-spotted;
   The living sky blue-spotted;
The living sky yellow-spotted;
The living sky white-spotted;
The young spruce as girls stood up for their
    dance in the way of life.
When my songs first were, they made my songs
    with words of jet.
Earth when it was made,
Sky when it was made,
Earth to the end,
Sky to the end,
Black gans, black thunder, when they came
    toward each other,
The various bad things that used to be vanished;
The bad wishes which were in the world vanished.
The lightning of the black thunder struck four
    times for them.
It struck four times for me.

EMERGENCE SONG (*Pima*)

TOGETHER we emerge with our rattles;
Together we emerge with our rattles,
Bright-hued feathers in our head-dresses.
    With our nyññyirsa we went down;
    With our nyññyirsa we went down,
    Wearing *Yoku* feathers in our head-dresses.
This is the white land; we arrive singing,
Head-dresses waving in the breeze.
We have come! We have come!
The land trembles with our dancing and singing.
  On these black mountains all are singing.
    Head-dresses waving, head-dresses waving.
    We all rejoice! We all rejoice!
    Singing, dancing, the mountains trembling.

THE WARNING OF THE FLOOD
(*Pima*)

WEEP my unfortunate people!
    All this you will see take place.
Weep my unfortunate people!
    For the waters will cover the land.
Weep my unhappy relatives!
    You will learn all.
Weep my unhappy relatives!
    You will learn all.
    The waters will cover the mountains.

Weep my unfortunate people!
    All this you will see take place.
Weep my unfortunate people!
    For the waters will cover the land.

PROTECTION SONG (*Navaho*)

I

Now, Slayer of the Alien Gods, among men am I.
Now among the alien gods with weapons
of magic am I.
Rubbed with the summits of the mountains,
Now among the alien gods with weapons of
magic am I.
Now upon the beautiful trail of old age,
Now among the alien gods with weapons of
magic am I.

II

Now, Offspring of the Water, among men am I.
Now among the alien gods with weapons of
magic am I.
Rubbed with the water of the summits,
Now among the alien gods with weapons of
magic am I.
Now upon the beautiful trail of old age,
Now among the alien gods with weapons of
magic am I.

III

Now, Lightning of the Thunder, among men
am I.

[99]

Now among the alien gods with weapons of
   magic am I.
Rubbed with the summit of the sky,
Now among the alien gods with weapons of
   magic am I.
Now upon the beautiful trail of old age,
Now among the alien gods with weapons of
   magic am I.

IV

Now, *Altsodoniglehi*, among men am I.
Now among the alien gods with weapons of
   magic am I.
Rubbed with the summits of the earth,
Now among the alien gods with weapons of
   magic am I.
Now upon the beautiful trail of old age,
Now among the alien gods with weapons of
   magic am I.

SONG OF NAYENEZGANI I (*Navaho*)

I

T HE Slayer of the Alien Gods,
That now am I.
The Bearer of the Sun
Arises with me,
Journeys with me,
Goes down with me,
Abides with me;
But sees me not.

II

Child of the Water
That now am I.
The Bearer of the Moon
Arises with me,
Journeys with me,
Goes down with me,
Abides with me;
But sees me not.

SONG OF NAYENEZGANI II
(*Navaho*)

I

I AM the Slayer of the Alien Gods,
   Where'er I roam
Before me
Forests white are strewn around.
The lightning scatters;
But 'tis I who cause it.

II

I am the Child of the Water.
Where'er I roam
Behind me
Waters white are strewn around.
The tempest scatters;
But 'tis I who cause it.

SONG OF THE HORSE (*Navaho*)

How joyous his neigh!
    Lo, the Turquoise Horse of Johano-ai,
    How joyous his neigh!
There on precious hides outspread standeth he;
    How joyous his neigh,
There on tips of fair fresh flowers feedeth he;
    How joyous his neigh,
There of mingled waters holy drinketh he;
    How joyous his neigh,
There he spurneth dust of glittering grains;
    How joyous his neigh,
There in mist of sacred pollen hidden, all hidden
        he;
    How joyous his neigh,
There his offspring many grow and thrive for
        evermore:
    How joyous his neigh!

SONG OF THE HOGANS (*Navaho*)

Lo, yonder the hogan,
    The hogan blessed!

There beneath the sunrise
    Standeth the hogan,
    The hogan blessed.

Of *Hastyeyalti-ye*
    The hogan,
    The hogan blessed.

Built of dawn's first light
    Standeth his hogan,
    The hogan blessed.

Built of fair white corn
    Standeth his hogan,
    The hogan blessed.

Built of broidered robes and hides
    Standeth his hogan,
    The hogan blessed.

Built of mixed All-Waters pure
    Standeth his hogan,
    The hogan blessed.

Built of holy pollen
    Standeth his hogan,
    The hogan blessed.

Evermore enduring,
Happy evermore,
        His hogan,
    The hogan blessed.

Lo, yonder the hogan,
    The hogan blessed!

There beneath the sunset
    Standeth the hogan,
    The hogan blessed.

Of *Hastyehogan-i*
    The hogan,
    The hogan blessed.

Built of afterglow
    Standeth his hogan,
    The hogan blessed.

Built of yellow corn
    Standeth his hogan,
    The hogan blessed.

Built of gems and shining shells
    Standeth his hogan,
    The hogan blessed.

Built of Little-Waters
    Standeth his hogan,
    The hogan blessed.

Built of holy pollen
    Standeth his hogan,
    The hogan blessed.

Evermore enduring,
Happy evermore,
    His hogan,
    The hogan blessed.

Lo, yonder the hogan,
    The hogan blessed!

WAR-SONG (*Navaho*)

Lo, the flint youth, he am I,
    The flint youth.

Nayenezrani, Lo, behold me, he am I,
    Lo, the flint youth, he am I,
        The flint youth.

Moccasins of black flint have I;
    Lo, the flint youth, he am I,
        The flint youth.

Leggings of black flint have I;
    Lo, the flint youth, he am I,
        The flint youth.

Tunic of black flint have I;
    Lo, the flint youth, he am I,
        The flint youth.

Bonnet of black flint have I;
    Lo, the flint youth, he am I,
        The flint youth.

Clearest, purest flint the heart
Living strong within me—heart of flint;
    Lo, the flint youth, he am I,
        The flint youth.

Now the zig-zag lightnings four
        From me flash,
Striking and returning,
        From me flash;
    Lo, the flint youth, he am I,
        The flint youth.

There where'er the lightnings strike,
Into the ground they hurl the foe—
Ancient folk with evil charms,
One upon another, dashed to earth;
    Lo, the flint youth, he am I,
        The flint youth.

Living evermore,
Feared of all forevermore,
    Lo, the flint youth, he am I,
        The flint youth.

Lo, the flint youth, he am I,
        The flint youth.

ATSÁLÈI YEDADIGLÉS (*Navaho*)

Now the holy one paints his form.
The Wind Boy, the holy one, paints his form,
All over his body, he paints his form,
With the dark clouds he paints his form,
With the misty rain he paints his form,
With the rainy bubbles he paints his form,
To fingers and rattle he paints his form,
To the plume on his head he paints his form.

MOUNTAIN SONGS (*Navaho*)

I

SWIFT and far I journey.
   Swift upon the rainbow.
Swift and far I journey.
Lo, yonder, the Holy Place!
      Yea, swift and far I journey.
To Sisnajinni, and beyond it,
      Yea, swift and far I journey;
The Chief of Mountains, and beyond it,
      Yea, swift and far I journey;
To Life Unending, and beyond it,
      Yea, swift and far I journey.

II

Homeward now shall I journey,
Homeward upon the rainbow;
Homeward now shall I journey,
Lo, yonder, the Holy Place!
      Yea, homeward now shall I journey.
To *Sisnajinni*, and beyond it,
      Yea, homeward now shall I journey;
The Chief of Mountains, and beyond it,
      Yea, homeward now shall I journey;

To Life Unending, and beyond it,
     Yea, homeward now shall I journey;
To Joy Unchanging, and beyond it,
     Yea, homeward now shall I journey.

III

Homeward behold me starting,
Homeward upon the rainbow;
Homeward behold me starting.
Lo, yonder, the Holy Place!
     Yea, homeward behold me starting.
To *Sisnajinni*, and beyond it,
     Yea, homeward behold me starting;
The Chief of Mountains, and beyond it,
     Yea, homeward behold me starting.
To Life Unending, and beyond it,
     Yea, homeward behold me starting;
To Joy Unchanging, and beyond it,
     Yea, homeward behold me starting.

IV

Homeward behold me faring,
Homeward upon the rainbow;
Homeward behold me faring.
Lo, yonder, the Holy Place!
     Yea, homeward behold me faring.
To *Sisnajinni*, and beyond it,
     Yea, homeward behold me faring;

The Chief of Mountains, and beyond it,
  Yea, homeward behold me faring;
To Life Unending, and beyond it,
  Yea, homeward behold me faring;
To Joy Unchanging, and beyond it,
  Yea, homeward behold me faring.

v

Now arrived home behold me,
Now arrived on the rainbow;
Now arrived home behold me,
Lo, here, the Holy Place!
  Yea, now arrived home behold me.
At *Sisnajinni*, and beyond it,
  Yea, now arrived home behold me;
The Chief of Mountains, and beyond it,
  Yea, now arrived home behold me;
In Life Unending, and beyond it,
  Yea, now arrived home behold me;
In Joy Unchanging, and beyond it,
  Yea, now arrived home behold me.

vi

Seated at home behold me,
Seated amid the rainbow;
Seated at home behold me,
Lo, here, the Holy Place!
  Yea, seated at home behold me.

At *Sisnajinni*, and beyond it,
       Yea, seated at home behold me;
The Chief of Mountains, and beyond it,
       Yea, seated at home behold me;
In Life Unending, and beyond it,
       Yea, seated at home behold me;
In Joy Unchanging, and beyond it,
       Yea, seated at home behold me.

MOUNTAIN SONG (*Navaho*)

I

In a holy place with a god I walk,
In a holy place with a god I walk,
On *Tsĭsnadzĭ'ni* with a god I walk,
On a chief of mountains with a god I walk,
In old age wandering with a god I walk.
On a trail of beauty with a god I walk.

II

In a holy place with a god I walk,
In a holy place with a god I walk,
On *Tsótsĭl* with a god I walk,
On a chief of mountains with a god I walk,
In old age wandering with a god I walk,
On a trail of beauty with a god I walk.

III

In a holy place with a god I walk,
In a holy place with a god I walk,
On *Dokoslíd* with a god I walk,
On a chief of mountains with a god I walk,
In old age wandering with a god I walk,
On a trail of beauty with a god I walk.

In a holy place with a god I walk,
In a holy place with a god I walk,
On *Depĕ'ntsa* with a god I walk,
On a chief of mountains with a god I walk,
In old age wandering with a god I walk,
On a trail of beauty with a god I walk.

MOUNTAIN SONG (*Navaho*)

Thither go I!
   Chief of all mountains,
Thither go I,
Living forever,
Thither go I,
Blessings bestowing.
Thither go I,
Calling me "Son, my son."
Thither go I.

INVOCATION OF THE GAME
(*San Ildefonso Pueblo*)

I
(North)

YONDER afar
By the Black Mountain
In the Valley
The Black Chief of the Elk is standing,
And he is our quarry.

II
(West)

Yonder afar
By the Mountain of Deer-Trails
In the Valley
The Yellow Chief of the Antelope is standing,
And hc is our quarry.

III
(South)

Yonder afar
By the Mountain of Flying
In the Valley
The Red Chief of the Antelope is standing,
And he is our quarry.

IV

(East)

Yonder afar
By the Mountain of Flowers
In the Valley
The White Chief of the Buffalo is standing,
And he is our quarry.

MEDICINE SONG (*Apache*)

STĕNÁTLĬHĂ^n, you are good, I pray for long life.
I pray for your good looks.
I pray for good breath.
I pray for good speech.
I pray for feet like yours to carry me through a
 long life.
I pray for a life like yours.
I walk with people; ahead of me all is well.
I pray for people to smile as long as I live.
I pray to live long.
I pray, I say, for a long life to live with you where
 the good people are.
I live in poverty.
I wish the people there to speak of goodness and
 and to talk to me.
I wish you to divide your good things with me
 as a brother.
Ahead of me is goodness; lead me on.

PRAYER OF THE FIRST
DANCERS (*Navaho*)

From the ceremony of the Night Chant

Iɴ *Tse'gihigi* (oh you who dwell!)
In the house made of the dawn,
In the house made of the evening twilight,
In the house made of the dark cloud,
In the house made of the he-rain,
In the house made of the dark mist,
In the house made of she-rain,
In the house made of pollen,
In the house made of grasshoppers,
Where the dark mist curtains the doorway,
The path to which is on the rainbow,
Where the zigzag lightning stands high on top,
Where the he-rain stands high on top,
Oh, male divinity!
With your moccasins of dark cloud, come to us.
With your leggings of dark cloud, come to us.
With your shirt of dark cloud, come to us.
With your head-dress of dark cloud, come to us.
With your mind enveloped in dark cloud, come
    to us.
With the dark thunder above you, come to us
    soaring.

With the shapen cloud at your feet, come to us
soaring.
With the far darkness made of the dark cloud
over your head, come to us soaring.
With the far darkness made of the he-rain over
your head, come to us soaring.
With the far darkness made of the dark mist
over your head, come to us soaring.
With the far darkness made of the she-rain over
your head, come to us soaring.
With the zigzag lightning flung out on high over
your head, come to us soaring.
With the rainbow hanging high over your head,
come to us soaring.
With the far darkness made of the dark cloud on
the ends of your wings, come to us soaring.
With the far darkness made of the he-rain on
the ends of your wings, come to us soaring.
With the far darkness made of the dark mist on
the ends of your wings, come to us soaring.
With the far darkness made of the she-rain on
the ends of your wings, come to us soaring.
With the zigzag lightning flung out on high on
the ends of your wings, come to us soaring.
With the rainbow hanging high on the ends of
your wings, come to us soaring.
With the near darkness made of the dark cloud,
of the he-rain, of the dark mist, and of the
she-rain, come to us.

With the darkness on the earth, come to us.
With these I wish the foam floating on the flow-
    ing water over the roots of the great corn.

I have made your sacrifice.
I have prepared a smoke for you.
My feet restore for me.
My limbs restore for me.
My body restore for me.
My mind restore for me.
My voice restore for me.
Today, take out your spell for me.
Today, take away your spell for me.
Away from me you have taken it.
Far off from me you have taken it.
Far off you have done it.
Happily I recover.
Happily my interior becomes cool.
Happily my eyes regain their power,
Happily my head becomes cool.
Happily my limbs regain their power.
Happily I hear again.
Happily for me (the spell) is taken off.
Happily I walk.
Impervious to pain, I walk.
Feeling light within, I walk.
With lively feelings, I walk.
Happily (or in beauty) abundant dark clouds
    I desire.

Happily abundant dark mists I desire.

Happily abundant passing showers I desire.

Happily an abundance of vegetation I desire.

Happily an abundance of pollen I desire.

Happily abundant dew I desire.

Happily may fair white corn, to the ends of the earth, come with you.

Happily may fair yellow corn, to the ends of the earth, come with you.

Happily may fair blue corn, to the ends of the earth, come with you.

Happily may fair corn of all kinds, to the ends of the earth, come with you.

Happily may fair plants of all kinds, to the ends of the earth, come with you.

Happily may fair goods of all kinds, to the ends of the earth, come with you.

Happily may fair jewels of all kinds, to the ends of the earth, come with you.

With these before you, happily may they come with you.

With these behind you, happily may they come with you.

With these below you, happily may they come with you.

With these above you, happily may they come with you.

With these all around you, happily may they come with you.

Thus happily you accomplish your task.
Happily the old men will regard you.
Happily the old women will regard you.
Happily the young men will regard you.
Happily the young women will regard you.
Happily the boys will regard you.
Happily the girls will regard you.
Happily the children will regard you.
Happily the chiefs will regard you.
Happily, as they scatter in different directions,
    they will regard you.
Happily, as they approach their homes, they
    will regard you.
Happily may their roads home be on the trail of
    pollen (peace).
Happily may they all get back.
In beauty (happily) I walk.
With beauty before me, I walk.
With beauty behind me, I walk.
With beauty below me, I walk.
With beauty above me, I walk.
With beauty all around me, I walk.
It is finished (again) in beauty,
It is finished in beauty,
It is finished in beauty,
It is finished in beauty.

A PRAYER OF THE SECOND DAY
OF THE NIGHT CHANT
(*Navaho*)

FROM the base of the east,
   From the base of the Pelado Peak,
From the house made of mirage,
From the story made of mirage,
From the doorway of rainbow,
The path out of which is the rainbow,
The rainbow passed out with me.
The rainbow raised up with me.
Through the middle of broad fields,
The rainbow returned with me.
To where my house is visible,
The rainbow returned with me.
To the roof of my house,
The rainbow returned with me.
To the entrance of my house,
The rainbow returned with me.
To just within my house,
The rainbow returned with me.
To my fireside,
The rainbow returned with me.
To the center of my house,
The rainbow returned with me.

At the fore part of my house with the dawn,
The Talking God sits with me.
The House God sits with me.
Pollen Boy sits with me.
Grasshopper Girl sits with me.
In beauty *Estsánatlehi*, my mother, for her I return.
Beautifully my fire to me is restored.
Beautifully my possessions are to me restored.
Beautifully my soft goods to me are restored.
Beautifully my hard goods to me are restored.
Beautifully my horses to me are restored.
Beautifully my sheep to me are restored.
Beautifully my old men to me are restored.
Beautifully my old women to me are restored.
Beautifully my young men to me are restored.
Beautifully my women are restored.
Beautifully my children to me are restored.
Beautifully my wife to me is restored.
Beautifully my chiefs to me are restored.
Beautifully my country to me is restored.
Beautifully my fields to me are restored.
Beautifully my house to me is restored.
Talking God sits with me.
House God sits with me.
Pollen Boy sits with me.
Grasshopper Girl sits with me.
Beautifully white corn to me is restored.
Beautifully yellow corn to me is restored.
Beautifully blue corn to me is restored.

Beautifully corn of all kinds to me is restored.
In beauty may I walk.
All day long may I walk.
Through the returning seasons may I walk.
Beautifully will I possess again.
On the trail marked with pollen may I walk.
With grasshoppers about my feet may I walk.
With dew about my feet may I walk.
With beauty may I walk.
With beauty before me, may I walk.
With beauty behind me, may I walk.
With beauty above me, may I walk.
With beauty below me, may I walk.
With beauty all around me, may I walk.
In old age wandering on a trail of beauty, lively,
    may I walk.
In old age wandering on a trail of beauty, living
    again, may I walk.
It is finished in beauty.
It is finished in beauty.

PRAYER TO DSILYI NEYÁNI
(*Navaho*)

R EARED Within the Mountains!
Lord of the Mountains!
Young Man!
Chieftain!
I have made your sacrifice.
I have prepared a smoke for you.
My feet restore thou for me.
My legs restore thou for me.
My body restore thou for me.
My mind restore thou for me.
My voice restore thou for me.
Restore all for me in beauty.
Make beautiful all that is before me.
Make beautiful all that is behind me.
Make beautiful my words.
It is done in beauty.
It is done in beauty.
It is done in beauty.
It is done in beauty.

DEDICATION OF A NEW HOUSE
(*Navaho*)

Man (*scattering white cornmeal about the circumfer-
ence of the room*):

MAY it be delightful, my house;
From my head may it be delightful;
To my feet may it be delightful;
Where I lie may it be delightful;
Above me may it be delightful;
All around me may it be delightful.

(*flinging meal into the fire*)
May it be delightful and well, my fire.

(*flinging meal up the smoke-hole*)
May it be delightful, Sun, my mother's
ancestor, for this gift;
May it be delightful as I walk around
my house.

(*sprinkling meal out the doorway*)
May it be delightful, this road of light
(the path of the Sun) my mother's
ancestor.

Woman (*making meal, offering to the fire, says quietly*):

> May it be delightful, my fire;
> May it be delightful for my children; may all be well;
> May it be delightful with my food and theirs; may all be well;
> All my possessions well may they be made.
> All my flocks well may they be made. (That is, may they all be healthy and increase.)

PRAYER OF THE FOSTER-PAR-
ENT CHANT (*Teton-Sioux*)

GREAT MYSTERY, you have existed from the first;
   This sky and this earth you created.
Wing flapper (Thunder Bird), you have existed
   from the first,
Your nation is half soldiers and half chiefs, so
   they say.
Lend me a good day; I borrow it.
Me, the Indian race, you have uplifted.
But now I am in despair;
Yet this good boy will renew the life of his people.
So, Great Mystery, look upon me; pity me,
That the nation may live—
Before the face of the North, the nation may live.

HOLY SONG (*Dakota*)

O YE people, be ye healed;
Life anew I bring unto ye.
O ye people, be ye healed;
Life anew I bring unto ye.
Through the Father over all
Do I thus.
Life anew I bring unto ye.

INVOKING THE VISIONS (*Pawnee*)

I

HOLY visions!
Hither come, we pray you, come unto us,
Bringing with you joy;
Come, O come to us, holy visions,
Bringing with you joy.

II

Holy visions!
Near are they approaching, near to us here,
Bringing with them joy;
Nearer still they come—holy visions—
Bringing with them joy.

III

Holy visions!
Lo! Before the doorway pause they, waiting,
Bearing gifts of joy;
Pausing there they wait—holy visions—
Bearing gifts of joy.

IV

Holy visions!
Now they cross the threshold, gliding softly

Toward the space within;
Softly gliding on—holy visions—
Toward the space within.

v

Holy visions!
They the lodge are filling with their presence,
Fraught with hope and peace;
Filling all the lodge—holy visions—
Fraught with hope and peace.

VI

Holy visions!
Now they touch the children, gently touch them,
Giving dreams of joy;
Gently touch each one—holy visions—
Giving dreams of joy.

VII

Holy visions!
Ended now their mission, pass they outward,
Yet they leave us joy;
Pass they all from us—holy visions—
Yet they leave us joy.

VIII

Holy visions!
They, the sky ascending, reach their dwelling;
There they rest above;
They their dwelling reach—holy visions—
There they rest above.

RITUAL SONG (*Pawnee*)

I

I KNOW not if the voice of man can reach to the
    sky;
I know not if the mighty one will hear as I pray;
I know not if the gifts I ask will all granted be;
I know not if the word of old we truly can hear;
I know not what will come to pass in our future
    days;
I hope that only good will come, my children, to
    you.

II

I now know that the voice of man can reach
    the sky;
I now know that the mighty one has heard as
    I prayed;
I now know that the gifts I asked have all granted
    been.
I now know that the word of old we truly have
    heard;
I now know that *Tirá wa* hearkens unto man's
    prayer;
I know that only good has come, my children,
    to you.

MEDICINE SONG (*Omaha*)

Ho! Aged One, *eçka*,
    At a time when there were gathered together
    seven persons,
You sat in the seventh place, it is said,
And of the Seven you alone possessed knowledge
    of all things,
Aged One, *eçka*.
When in their longing for protection and guid-
    ance,
The people sought in their minds for a way,
They beheld you sitting with assured permanency
    and endurance
In the center where converged the paths,
There, exposed to the violence of the four winds,
    you sat,
Possessed with power to receive supplications,
Aged One, *eçka*.
Where is his mouth, by which there may be
    utterance of speech?
Where is his heart, to which there may come
    knowledge and understanding?
Where are his feet, whereby he may move from
    place to place?
We question in wonder,

Yet verily it is said you alone have power to
　　receive supplications,
Aged One, *eçka*.
I have desired to go yet farther in the path of
　　life with my little ones,
Without pain, without sickness,
Beyond the second, third, and fourth period of
　　life's pathway,
Aged One, *eçka*.
O hear! This is my prayer,
Although uttered in words poorly put together,
Aged One, *eçka*.

SONG OF THE PRIMAL ROCK
(*Omaha*)

O H! Aged One, *eçka*,
  Oh! thou recumbent Rock, *eçka*,
Aged One, *eçka*,
To thee I shall pray, *eçka*,
Aged One, *eçka*,
Oh! Aged One, *eçka*,
The great water that lies impossible to traverse,
  eçka,
Aged One, *eçka*,
In the midst of the waters thou came and sat,
  eçka,
Aged One, *eçka*,
Thou, of whom one may think, whence camest
  thou? *eçka*,
Aged One, *eçka*,
From midst the waters camest thou, and sat, *eçka*.
It is said that thou sittest crying: "I^n! I^n! *eçka*,
Though I shall carry these my little ones, *eçka*,
Though I shall sit and listen to their words, *eçka*,
Because," they say, you have said, *eçka*,
"If one shall go astray in his speech, although
  here lies one on whom one's footsteps may
  seem impossible to stumble, *eçka*,

Upon this, the earth, very suddenly he shall
    stumble," they say you have said, *eçka*,
Aged One, *eçka*,
The impurities, *eçka*,
Shall not enter within, *eçka*,
Shall drift, like filth, as thou sittest, *eçka*,
Aged One, *eçka*
Oh! Aged One, *eçka*,
"If one of mine prays to me properly,"*eçka*,
Aged One, *eçka*,
"I shall be with him, *eçka*,
Further along he shall go,"*eçka*.
Aged One, *eçka*,
"The fourth hill, *eçka*,
The third, the fourth, *eçka*,
Even in going they shall appear thereon," they
    say you have said, *eçka*,
Aged One, *eçka*,
Oh! Aged One, *eçka*,
Thou sittest as though longing for something,
    eçka,
Thou sittest like one with wrinkled loins, *eçka*,
Thou sittest like one with furrowed brow, *eçka*,
Thou sittest like one with flabby arms, *eçka*,
"The little ones shall be as I am, whoever shall
    pray to me properly," *eçka*,
Oh! Aged One, *eçka*,
Oh! Thou Pole of the Tent, *eçka*,
Along the banks of the streams, *eçka*,

With head drooping over, there thou sittest,
 eçka,
Thy topmost branches, *eçka*,
Dipping again and again, verily, into the water,
 eçka,
Thou Pole of the Tent, *eçka*,
"One of these little ones, *eçka*,
I shall sit upon one, *eçka*,
The impurities, *eçka*,
All I shall wash away from them, *eçka*,
To the end, without one obstacle, they shall ap-
 pear thereon," they say you have said, *eçka*,
Aged One, *eçka*,
It is said that you have commanded us to say
 to you, "Our Father, *eçka*,
Thou Water, *eçka*,
Oh! Along the bends of the stream where the
 waters strike, and where the waters eddy,
 among the water-mosses, let all the impur-
 ities that gall be drifted, *eçka*,
Not entering within," *eçka*.
Aged One, *eçka*,
"Whosoever touches me with face or lips, *eçka*,
All the impurities, *eçka*,
I shall cause to be cleansed," it is said, you have
 said, *eçka*.
"The four apertures of the body, *eçka*,
And all within the body I shall purify," it is
 said, you have said, *eçka*.

"Little ones, *eçka*,
Through and through shall appear, *eçka*,
Against the wind, in the midst of air, they shall
    appear and stand," *eçka*,
It is said you have said, *eçka*,
Aged One, *eçka*.

INTRODUCTION OF THE CHILD
TO THE COSMOS (*Omaha*)

I

Ho! Ye Sun, Moon, Stars, all ye that move
  in the heavens,
  I bid you hear me!
Into your midst has come a new life.
  Consent ye, I implore!
Make its path smooth, that it may reach the
  brow of the first hill!

II

Ho! Ye Winds, Clouds, Rain, Mist, all ye that
  move in the air,
  I bid ye hear me!
Into your midst has come a new life.
  Consent ye, I implore!
Make its path smooth, that it may reach the
  brow of the second hill!

III

Ho! Ye Hills, Valleys, Rivers, Lakes, Trees,
  Grasses, all ye of the earth,
  I bid you hear me!

Into your midst has come a new life.
     Consent ye, I implore!
Make its path smooth, that it may reach the
     brow of the third hill!

IV

Ho! Ye Birds, great and small, that fly in the air,
Ho! Ye Animals, great and small, that dwell in
     the forest,
Ho! Ye Insects that creep among the grasses
     and burrow in the ground,
     I bid you hear me!
Into your midst has come a new life.
     Consent ye, I implore!
Make its path smooth, that it may reach the
     brow of the fourth hill!

V

Ho! All ye of the heavens, all ye of the air, all
     ye of the earth,
     I bid you all to hear me.
Into your midst has come a new life.
     Consent ye, consent ye all, I implore!
Make its path smooth—then shall it travel be-
     yond the four hills!

SONG OF TURNING THE CHILD
(Omaha)

I

Ye four, come hither and stand, near shall ye
   stand;
In four groups shall ye stand;
Here shall ye stand, in this place stand.

II

Turned by the winds goes the one I send yonder;
Yonder he goes who is whirled by the winds;
Goes, where the four hills of life and the four
   winds are standing;
There, in the midst of the winds do I send him,
Into the midst of the winds, standing there.

III

Here unto you has been spoken the truth;
Because of this truth you shall stand.
Here, declared is the truth.
Here in this place has been shown you the truth.
Therefore, arise! Go forth in its strength!

SUPPLICATION OF THE TSÍZHU
WASHTÁGE (*Osage*)

WAKONDA will cause the coming days to be calm
and peaceful,
The Tsízhu have called upon Wakonda to make
the days calm and peaceful,
That little ones may come to us in unbroken
succession and we become a people.
Wakonda will make the days beautiful.
Toward the winds of the rising of the sun the
days will surely be calm and peaceful.
Toward the winds of the south Wakonda will
make the days to be calm and peaceful.
Toward the winds of the setting sun Wakonda
will make the days to be calm and peaceful.
Toward the winds of the land of cedars (the
north) Wakonda will make the days to be
calm and peaceful.

THE TRIBAL PRAYER (*Omaha*)

FATHER, a needy one before Thee stands.
I am he!

WAWAN SONG *(Omaha)*

THE clear sky,
 The green fruitful earth is good;
But peace among men is better.

THE MORNING SONG (*Cheyenne*)

He, our Father,
He hath shown His mercy unto me.
In peace I walk the straight road.

PART TWO

Poetic Forms in American Indian Lyrics

POETIC FORMS IN AMERICAN
INDIAN LYRICS

*T*HE true touchstone of primitive verse is
familiarity with aboriginal life and manners.
Let the observer sit among the American Indians
under a starlit sky in the far spaces of the
desert, or with his horizon bound by native
forests, where only blazed trails penetrate the
shadows—wherever these people sing, encircling
a quiet fire. Not even the folk-songs of the
colored race on their native plantations con-
vey the sense of detached unreality that comes
with hearing these evening songs of the red
race.

When a thousand songs have beaten their
way into his pulse, the listener may hope to
understand both the form and the spirit of this
verse. Only this certain recognition acquired
by personal knowledge can direct him to sound
judgments of the current pseudo-Indian verse.
It is the only safe basis for comparison when
studies lead far afield into the song-literature of
many tribes. Many of us, however, cannot
readily explore the remote places of aboriginal
song. For such readers, fortunately, there is

an increasing number of printed studies and of records gathered by our great museums.

Even after wide observation and the close study of years, many questions will still remain to baffle us. To reconcile many apparent inconsistencies of Indian lyric verse forms, we must first understand the *thought-movement* of this body of poetry before we approach the whole subject of *thought-rhythm*, with the questions of *repetition* and of *stanzaic* and *metrical structure*.

In the mood of the poet, to be sure, lies the chief influence which shapes the poem and marks its larger formal characteristics of thought-movement and rhythm. There are the graceful, lilting verses that go swiftly to the golden melodies of some of the shorter lyrics, as in the *Song of the Coyote and Locust*; others which move in slow processional to stately chants, as in the odes of *The Night Chant*.

But the thought-movement is the more immediate influence upon the structure of a poem. The pre-eminently characteristic movement of the Indian lyric is recessional.[1] It perceptibly intensifies the haunting, melancholy effect in which the lyric usually finds voice. The *motif* appears at the opening of the song, with emotional intensity or emphasis gradually dying away toward the close. This movement commonly occurs in the shorter songs which are entirely repeated several times. This recessional movement is effective with its musical accompaniment, repeating the melody in a descending scale, and ending on a low note. Thus *pitch* and *accent*, as well as varying *quantity*, mark the repetitions and lessen their monotony.

As a modification of the recessional movement, there is the poem which opens with the *motif* and repeats it at regularly recurring points throughout, concluding abruptly without the refrain. There are some stanzaic units in this group. Whatever may be the gain in emphasis and in organization, there is a distinct loss in atmosphere. This type is interesting as a transitional stage.

The second type of thought-movement has influenced a third group of songs which shows wide divergence from the first. In this last group the major emphasis always opens and closes the song, though it recurs at intervals, as at the opening or close of each stanza. This is the most finished lyric in design, the most completely thought out, with stanzaic units distinct. Mood and idea join to create a beautiful form.

To a less extent, the processional, or forward, thought-movement appears in lyric form. It may progress toward an emotional climax at the end of a song or a sequence. In the songs before sunrise, as the *Daylight Song* in *The Hako*, the intensity increases toward the close as dawn appears. The forward movement finds its most natural place in the ballads and in those ritualistic poems which anticipate dramatic gesture or action. This dramatic relationship, whether in formal ceremony or in vocational songs, shapes the thought-movement in direct contrast to the characteristic order.

There are other poems which carry the thought forward to the close, rounding with an effective summary, sustaining the heightened interest, yet showing the fine intellectual perception of form in relation to thought which appears in *Mount Koonak: A Song of Arsut*. In characteristics, this type approaches the lyric which Doctor Moulton has classified as the *free sonnet*.

Whatever variations appear in the sequence of thought, it must be remembered that the use of the recessional movement is a primary law of Indian lyric art.

There is within the lyric a sense of symmetry, of poetic consistency, which cannot be measured by Anglo-Saxon rules of prosody. The Indian poet achieves this symmetry in structure by using varied patterns of thought-rhythm; that is, by means of infinitely modified forms of repetition which are as distinctively characteristic of his genius as parallelism was of the ancient Hebrew or as the variations of rhyme and of stanzaic pattern are of the English lyric genius of the last four centuries. The subtle relationship of patterns of thought-rhythm to the whole movement of a poem is often so fugitive as to escape analysis. One origin of these patterns is the most obvious dramatic association which may also determine the direction of the entire thought-movement. Although the dramatic *motif* shapes both aspects of thought, there is no apparent connection between the progression of an idea and, let us say, the alternating rhythm, except when the alternation becomes incremental. The determining values of pitch and of melodic repetition are also important external factors. Where these influences end, it is difficult to say.

So far as this study has proceeded, five characteristic patterns of thought-rhythm appear in Indian lyric poetry. The iterative rhythm appears in the simpler poems, of which the Navaho *Mountain Song* and *The Omaha Tribal Prayer* are particularly fine in spirit. The iteration is not always pleasing, sometimes beating with the steady monotony of a kettle drum; but, contrary to reasonable supposition, it does not necessarily indicate a dance song.

The alternating rhythm offers the Indian

poet some æsthetic relief. It creates a graceful lilt in his verse and often accompanies the quicker movements. This is a universal pattern; but some *Katzina Songs* of the Hopi and songs of the Zuñi and Pima Indians have markedly achieved this freedom of movement. The elasticity of this form provides an infinite variety of uses, from carrying a pleasant refrain to providing a choric response for the support of a dancing soloist. It has a place in the vocational songs, as well as in the ritual songs of a tribe. There are many variants which employ alternating patterns of thought at the opening and close of a stanza, or with dramatic pose and gesture, as in the Zuñi *Invocation to the Sun-God*, in singing which the Indian mother appeals to the sun, moon, and stars to guide her sleeping infant. Mr. Troyer marks the values of pitch as heightening the rhythmic movements of this song.

Balanced forms of thought, that is, forms in parallel structure, do not appear commonly. Perhaps it is more exact to recall that pure iteration and alternation of thought approximate the effects which parallelism may contribute, especially when the repetition is sung in a different pitch from that of the key thought. The infrequent occurrence of sharp contrasts of imagery, or antitheses of thought, may explain the rare use of parallelism. The ancient lament of the Onondagas, preserved in *The Iroquois Book of Rites*, remains one of the most beautifully wrought poems of this type brought down to our time.

The interlacing design of thought is one of the most graceful as well as one of the most difficult. This pattern shows skill and delicacy in poetic construction, as the interlacing repetitions frequently carry from one stanza to another, as from first to third and second to fourth, found in *The Morning Star and the New Born Dawn*, from *The Hako*. This device carries the thought forward. It is, therefore, definitely related in purpose to the form which is universally the vehicle of the ballad—incremental repetition. The Indian poet uses this form both for narrative and for descriptive purposes. The Navaho *Song of the Horse* shows a studied picture, framing each detail with repetitions; while the same incremental use of repetition carries forward the narrative in the *Navaho Rain Chant*.

There is a further structural use of these forms. If we can point to a single prototype of the lyric stanza, we must find it in the unit of thought-rhythm. As it assumed different aspects, enlarging itself with repetitions, there appeared the first conscious step, the stanzaic germ with varying possibilities of structure. This æsthetic

origin of the stanza appeared before the intellectual recognition of unity of thought.   In
this song recorded by Miss Fletcher, there is a
stanzaic germ of typically primitive quality.
It is lengthened, possibly, for singing.   The
composer shaped three words into the form of
a stanza by the use of repetitions and the addition of vocables.

> *No^n-we shka-dse, no^n-we shka-dse;*
> Ha-ha! e he tha, Ha-ha! we
> Ha-ha! e he tha.
> Ha-ha! e he tha tha. *Ho-ga!*
> *No^n-we shka-dse, no^n-we shka-dse;*
> Ha-ha! e he tha.

In countless song-poems, however, the compact-
ness of thought and swift unity of impression have
evolved stanzas with complex and studied patterns
of thought-rhythm.

Other distinct influences over the varying
patterns of the stanza are the mystic numbers
and the dramatic element in the ceremonials,
the former more often determining the length
of the stanzas and the number of such divisions
in a song.   The ritualistic use of the numbers
two, three, four, five, six, seven, and occasionally
of multiples of these numbers, determines the
number of stanzas and repetitions in ritualistic
songs.   It is rather unusual to find distinct

tribal preferences in the number of song divisions; although the Taos Pueblo uses two parts and the Blackfoot tribe often seven. Orientation to the world quarters has almost universally established some use of four stanzas and four repetitions in religious songs. Dramatic influence emphasizes the fourfold division, especially in the ritual.

The length of the stanza at no point appears as fixed as the number of stanzas and repetitions. The stanzaic pattern repeats itself exactly more often in a ritual song than in a secular. Many of the odes have extremely long stanzas, some units of thought reaching to one hundred lines, as the *Prayer of the First Dancers* in the Navaho *Night Chant*. The length of the stanza in other songs may range from the distich to the sixteen line unit, although little stanzas of three to six lines appear to be the most pleasing to the Indian poet. The longer stanzas commonly employ preludes and refrains and at times resort to repetition of matter.

The oral lyric makes certain special demands of the composer. There must be devices for marking off the stanzas. In addition to certain formal patterns of repetition, these devices include tag endings, such as conclude the scenes in Elizabethan drama, endings with a sharp contrast in pitch and care in enunciation. The drop in pitch appears at the close of the unit of music corresponding to the unit of verse. There may occur, also, a complete change of rhythm and a distinct change in thought from stanza to stanza. Cycles of short songs, or song-sequences with fixed repetitions in the ceremonials, give the effect of stanzaic divisions. We must conclude that the lack of written or printed forms appears no hindrance to the development of stanzaic patterns.

The question of rhyme schemes invites more attention than some other markers of the stanza. It is, to be sure, a relatively unimportant factor in Indian rhythms: although the wide use of assonance commonly approximates rhyme, and elaborate schemes of repetition serve a like purpose. Various schemes of rhyme are used in the songs of *The Night Chant*, particularly in the internal and end rhymes. In the *Song of the Meal Rubbing*[1] the second element in the internal rhyme scheme binds the lines together:

> Bĭtsísi . . . .
> Estsanatléhisi . . . .
> Alkaíye . . . .
> Bikenagádbe . . . .
> Bitalataibe . . . .
> Bĭdató'be . . . .
> Biselataíbe . . . .
> Bĭthadítínbe . . . .

Bǐdetsébe . . . .
Sána-nogaíbe . . . .
Biké-hozóbe . . . .

A simpler and more characteristic internal rhyme
scheme is found in the *Prayer of the First Dancers*,[2]
aaa bbb, in lines 14 to 21:

. . . .nǐkégo. . . .
. . . .nǐsklégo. . . .
. . . .niégo. . . .
. . . .nitságo. . . .
. . . .bininǐnlágo. . . .
. . . .dahitágo. . . .

Two further illustrations show the Navaho command of end rhymes. In the *Daylight Song*,[3]
there is easy inversion of pattern, *abba:*

. . . .dóla aní,
. . . .bǐza holó,
. . . .bǐza hozó,
. . . .hwí he inlí.

In *Slayer of the Alien Gods*,[4] the rhyme *aaaaa*
achieves a definite tone color, rounding with a
full open syllable:

. . . .sǐnǐsnlígo,
. . . .hánatahasgo,
. . . .nítatahasgo,
. . . .ínatahasgo,
. . . .nínatahasgo.

We must keep in mind that these uses of rhyme serve only a secondary purpose in drawing together the elements of the pattern within the stanza.

The stanza of Indian verse, it readily appears, is flexible in form—both in length of line and in length of thought-unit. The rapid tempo exploys a short line, as in this Maliseet *Dance-Song:* [1]

> Kive-hiu-wha-ni-ho
> Ya hi ye
> Kive-hiu-wha-ni-yo
> Ya hi ye
> Ya hi ye
> Kshi-te-ka-mo-tik'lo
> Ya hi ye
> Ya hi ye
> Pilsh-kwe-sis-tok'lo
> Ya hi ye
> Kshi-te-ka-mo-tik'lo
> Ya hi ye
> Twa, twa, twa, twa!

The short line does not merely accompany rapid movement. It appears a measure of severe economy in some prayers in which the Indian catalogs his daily needs for seventy or more lines! The formal invocations, however, commonly use the longer line and the slower movement. Long, slow, even lines breathe the lament of the *Death of Taluta* and the reflective cadences of *Mount Koonak: A Song of Arsut*.

The variation of the lyric line shows technical skill. The *Dance-Song* just quoted beats out only a simple alteration of long and short lines. *The Song of the Coyote and the Locust* begins with long flowing lines, but snaps off with a gay quick ending:

> Tchumali, tchumali, shohkoya,
> Tchumali, tchumali, shohkoya,
> Yaamii heeshoo taatani tchupatchiute
> > Shohkoya,
> > Shohkoya!

When the shorter line falls within the stanza, there is greater play of mood and thought, with the elasticity of the outward swing and return in the rhythm of the thought as we feel it through the succession of stanzas in *The Song of the Rain Chant*. The line of verse sweeps outward and the thought recedes at the ebb, as clearly as a *Hiroshige* wave crest lifts and the waters return to their level.

Within the silhouette of the verse are indisputable metrical patterns, some structural, some decorative. These patterns frequently occur in phrases; and these phrases, in turn, fall into a larger pattern which may be repeated or may be

interchanged with other patterns of corresponding values. They are sometimes of amazing com-
plexity, yet form a compact unity of design.

Few correspondences appear in the versification of the white race; but the Indians' use of
pitch [1] for marking off rhythmic units is similar
to such a use in Chinese poetry. For analysis,
we must observe native singers and study phonographic records. The printed verse gives little
opportunity for the study of meter except through
musical accompaniment, when the phrases of
the music and of the verse coincide, as few notable
investigators have set down accent and quantity.
Only phonographic records show the use of
pitch in rhythm, an element most familiar to
any one who has ever heard the Indians chant
and sing. Two related arts explain the unique
character of Indian lyric measures, the musical
setting and the oral rendition of the poem.

Miss Natalie Curtis once asked an Indian singer,
"Which came first, the words or the music?"

"They came at the same moment," he answered.

We must accept that explanation for the
choicest lyrics: yet we cannot, in that way,
account for some performances of remarkable
ingenuity. A singer with the art of a counter-
puntist may subordinate the iambic word-rhythm
of his poem to an alternating three-four and
two-four rhythm of the melody, while he dances

at the same moment to the unaccented rhythm
of the drum. The whole question turns again
in his next song in which he faithfully sets the
lilt of his verse to the corresponding rhythm
of the music. Any first hand comparison of the
word-rhythm and the melodic rhythm proceeds
with the greatest difficulty. Since the Indian
invariably sings the lyrics, often many times, before dictating the words, he tends to employ the
melodic rhythm in speaking the lines.

It is possible, of course, that the shifting of
natural speech stresses to adapt the verse to the
music marks the distinct composition of words
and of music, with the latter as the earlier effort.
There can be no doubt that, in aboriginal life,
music is more generally persistent than words,
and that new verses sometimes replace forgotten songs. On the other hand, it is equally
certain that many of these misfit songs are only
inferior compositions, hobbling in their meter
just as the white poet's lyrics at times go halt-
ingly in their rhythm.

Whether the Indian poet composed his lyric
and melody simultaneously or composed the
verse to the rhythm of the melody, he conceived
his song as an oral expression which should set
free his mood through an interpretive accompaniment. That some melodies have changed
their verbal associations in the history of cen-

turies may indicate that new experiences have informed their characteristic rhythms. If the original words have been lost, it is entirely possible that the new poem is perfectly adjusted to the music as a genuine re-expression of the rhythm and sweep of the melody. We have a notable instance in English in the poetry of Burns.

Indian lyric poetry has, we have noted, the qualities of oral verse. It employs a number of devices to mark off rhythmic units: stress, accent, range in pitch, quantity, and effort in enunciation. Stress and the higher pitch coincide almost universally. The dramatic and the musical influence require some use of quantity. Aside from its main use in the tag ending of verse or stanza when stress is not used for that purpose, effort in enunciation appears to be an accidental rhythmic element, depending upon the use of the high, close vowels, as e, and the aspirated, closed, and guttural consonants. It is, therefore, least useful when it coincides with the other devices of rhythm—lost, as it must be, in the use of stress. Indian poetry makes a sharp distinction, it must be observed, between accent and stress, the latter requiring definite bodily effort, even explosive enunciation.

The oral rendition of a poem brings us to some unexpected turns in versification. A scholar observes that one must have an Indian throat to sing these songs. This physical control is two fold: unique control of the breathing and contraction or pulsation of the glottis, especially in measures of unusual length. In Indian verse, there is a lengthening of the metrical unit beyond the ordinary limits of European verse in feet of six, seven, eight, and nine syllables, with but one syllable prominent in stress, pitch, or quantity. The Indian sings and speaks on for hours without apparent weariness.

The elemental two and three syllabled feet appear universally in Indian poetry, but commonly in phrases with the longer feet of five to nine syllables, as in the *Pledge Song* of the Chippewa: *nin-da-ca-mi-gog | éya*. Another pattern has the recurring metrical phrase of three, six, and five syllables: *i e ba | bá-pi-ni-si-wa-gûn | gé-non-de-ci-nan*. A rhythmic group of five and one may be varied by the substitution of a three syllabled and a two syllabled measure for that of five syllables. A song may carry a two syllabled rhythm consistently, even when all repetitions of line are disregarded:

> O kú wah tsá, úm weh dah án,
> Hang wén bo wú u wán moon pí,
> Han wán bo hí wut di ún wéh dah án,
> É yan ne *yá* ah né yáh na án.
> Ah é yan ne yáh ah né yáh na án.

A Papago harvest song, for instance, balances high and low pitched measures in rising three syllabled rhythm, which suggests a dance with gesture or swaying of the body. In each phrase of the song, the foot of the higher pitch carries the heavier stress. This double use of pitch and stress, or accent, in phrases of two measures runs throughout the song, showing the regularity of metrical pattern to be expected where the lyric accompanies action or ritual observance. Such definite schemes of short measures do not appear as commonly as in English lyric poetry. In many Indian lyrics there is a tendency to avoid such emphatic rhythms—a tendency toward the free rhythms, though the sense of measure is never lost. On the whole, Indian lyric poetry is highly rhythmical in structure, although not closely metrical.

The most interesting metrical patterns are the long units which almost escape the ear as they die away in the low pitched glottal vibrations of a glide. In these measures, liquid consonants frequently combine with open vowels; though a Chippewa singer may take *b*, *t*, *g*, and *k* in one long unit. The singer finds the feet of eight and nine syllables easiest when they are made up of vocables or of elongations of a syllable, as *e-ye-e-e-e-e-e-e-e-*, receding in delicate sound waves and requiring no effort in enunciation. These sound waves may occur as a scarcely perceptible double pulsation within the long unit, in such syllables as *e-ya*, *ai-ya*, which require little articulation. The poet can sing them indefinitely, as they fall into the rhythm of respiration. This syllabic group is the irreducible unit within the foot; if we eliminate the lengthening of a vowel, a device for the singer rather than for the poet.

The function of the vocable in the metrical design is nonessential from the intellectual viewpoint; but there is a clear value, from an æsthetic viewpoint, in the full rounded vowels of many syllables. They give tone color to the whole song, and enrich the metrical design.

The range in metrical patterns gives infinite variety and freedom to Indian verse. The poet varies even his repetition of rhythmic phrases by using different degrees of pitch. By far the most notable element in Indian versification, in fact, is this art of combining dissimilar rhythms and of playing one against another with the effect of many instruments.

All the subtlety of charm and melody in the verse evades analysis in the study of rhythms; yet poetry is no less beautiful because we catch the grace of a flowing line and the play of assonance through open syllables, as in the Zuñi *Sunset Song;* the contrasting gaiety of light, quick, staccato movement; or the faultless symmetry of antiphonals. It is extremely difficult to interpret in terms of occidental prosody the poetic genius which arose from an alien civilization. We must constantly return to our cultural backgrounds for explanation.

It is not an incidental play-motif that the Zuñi children sing in the *Hymn to the Sun*, "Listen, just listen," as they hold spiral shells to their ears. Mr. Troyer wrote: "The primary aim seems to be to develop early in life, by mechanical aids, the perception of solar vibration, which later in life becomes a natural gift." A critic whose hearing is less sensitive than that of the Red Man will remain wholly unaware of many delicate nuances.

These subtle changes in Indian lyrics can scarcely be said to follow metrical laws, yet cannot be thought accidental. The shifting influence of pause is negligible. There is slight use of quantity except in vocalic and consonantal interplay, and that is most elusive. Subtleties of mood and thought in the line may turn swiftly from the flowing movement to the staccato with corresponding shift in measure. A distinct influence appears in the cluster-rhythms of holophrastic compounds. This element becomes especially noticeable when the singer pauses to dictate the words of his song. The crest words or syllables in a line, particularly in the recessional movement and in descending pitch, may also shift the metrical emphasis. In the Zuñi song *Lover's Wooing*, the crest words are most distinct: blanket, maiden, awaiting, alone, walk, come. The rhythm bends to them.

To one who has listened to countless Indian songs, there remains another logical influence over the exquisite variations of these lyrics—mimesis of elements of the natural world. The rhythms of nature float through the rhythms of Indian verse. The winds are imitated in the oral rendition of many poems: the minor key, the little rushes of wind, the full swell of sound, the gradual dying away. Curiously enough, the Plains tribes call their songs in recollection of the absent "wind songs," in true appreciation of their minor key.

The steady patter or downfall of rain sings a welcome rhythm to the Indian of the plains and of the southwest. There is an insistence in the rhythm of many rain-songs that is mimetic, not only in the total effect of rain but distinctly so in the character of metrical units. "I like those songs," an old man once said to me quite simply, his face quickened with a smile. His songs had just measured the summer rain, then dropped away through gliding syllables to a whispering echo—the wind and the rain!

It is the natural, joyous response of the Red Man to his surroundings that catches up these free rhythms of the out-door world and shapes his gesture and thought in measure with them in his improvisations. In the subtlety of its rhythms, Indian lyric poetry cannot detach itself from these external influences; for no race of the modern world lives more intimately with nature, sensing its most delicate expressions, its most exquisite sounds and movements.

These natural rhythms, though constantly recurring, may appear largely incidental; yet there are elemental laws at work determining lyric rhythms, laws we must seek behind the poetic impulse. One law is that poetic art, as all other arts, shall be rooted fast in the physical surroundings which temper the race. Any effort to wrest an art from that traditional environment breaks it off at the tap root.

NOTES

21. Burton, Frederick. American Primitive Music. Part II, p. 1. An interpretation. Moffat, Yard. N. Y. 1909. (Now published by Dodd, Mead, N. Y.)
22. *Ibid.*, Part II, pp. 29–30. An interpretation. The Princess Tsianina includes this song in her repertory.
23. Troyer, Carlos. Traditional Songs of the Zuñi. Theodore Presser. Philadelphia.
25. Austin, Mary. The American Rhythm, p. 88. Harcourt, Brace & Co., N. Y. 1923.
26. Curtis, Natalie. The Indians' Book, p. 57. Harpers. N. Y. 1923.
27. Leland, Charles G. Algonquin Legends of New England, p. 318. Houghton, Mifflin. Boston. 1884.
28. Burton, Frederick. American Primitive Music, Part II, p. 11. An interpretation.
29. Curtis, Natalie. The Indians' Book, p. 50.
30. Hale, Horatio. The Iroquois Book of Rites, pp. 153–154. Library of Aboriginal Literature. Philadelphia. 1883.
31. Austin, Mary. Harper's Magazine, Vol. 143, p. 78. (June, 1921). *See also* The American Rhythm, p. 84.
32. Eastman, Charles A. Old Indian Days, p. 32. McClure. N. Y. 1907. (Now published by Little, Brown, Boston.)

33. Curtis, Natalie. The Indians' Book, p. 317.
34. *Ibid.*, p. 225.
35. Riggs, A. L. Dakota Songs and Music: Tâh-koo Wa-kân, p. 462. Boston. 1869.
36. Dorsey, J. Owen. The Cegiha Language, p. 611. Bur. of Amer. Eth. Washington. 1890.
37. Spinden, H. J. Home Songs of the Tewa Indians, p. 78. The American Museum Journal. Amer. Mus. of Nat. Hist. N. Y. vol. XV, no. 2.
38. *Ibid.*, p. 73.
39. Curtis, Natalie. The Indians' Book, p. 370.
41. Goddard, Pliny Earle. Myths and Tales of the San Carlos Apache, p. 62. American Museum of Natural History. N. Y. 1918.
42. Rink, Henry. Tales and Traditions of the Eskimo, pp. 68–69. Blackwood. London. 1875.
43. Cushing, Frank. Zuñi Folk Tales, p. 255. Putnam's. N. Y. 1901.
44. Powell, James. Mythology of North American Indians, p. 23. Bur. of Amer. Eth. Washington. 1881.
45. Curtis, Natalie. The Indians' Book, p. 462.
46. Fletcher, Alice C. The Hako, p. 303. Bur. of Amer. Eth. Washington. 1904.
47. *Ibid.*, pp. 305–306.
48. *Ibid.*, p. 342.
49. Curtis, Natalie. The Indians' Book, p. 317.
50. Densmore, Frances. Chippewa Music II, p. 254. Bur. of Amer. Eth. Washington. 1913.
51. Converse, Harriet Maxwell. Myths and Legends of the New York State Iroquois, pp. 180–183. New York State Museum. 1908.

56. La Flesche, Francis. The Osage Tribe, pp. 295–296. 36th Ann. Rep. Bur. of Amer. Eth. Washington. 1921. In this poem, each line represents a complete stanza in the original—a stanza built up of repetitions and vocables.

57. Curtis, Natalie. The Indians' Book, pp. 365–366.

59. Matthews, Washington. Navaho Legends, p. 27. Houghton, Mifflin. N. Y. 1877. For the American Folk Lore Society.

60. Corbin, Alice. Red Earth, pp. 27–28, with note on p. 57. R. F. Seymour. Chicago. 1920.

62. Curtis, Natalie. The Indians' Book, p. 432.

63. *Ibid.*, p. 431.

64. *Ibid.*, p. 432.

65. *Ibid.*, p. 484–485.

66. *Ibid.*, p. 483.

67. *Ibid.*, p. 485.

68. *Ibid.*, p. 479. Muyinga is the god of germination and growth.

69. Stevenson, Matilda Coxe. The Sia, p. 124. Bur. of Amer. Eth. Washington. 1896.

70. *Ibid.*, p. 124. *See also* Mrs. Austin's "Rain Songs from the Rio Grande Pueblos" in The American Rhythm, pp. 92–94.

71. Russell, Frank. The Pima Indians, pp. 333–334. Bur. of Amer. Eth. Washington. 1904–1905. "The first songs ever sung to bring rain. *Hooni* was the name of the Corn God who left the Pimas for many years and then returned to live at the mountain north of Picacho, Ta-atukam, whence he sang as above."

73. *Ibid.*, pp. 331–333. The vivid imagery of the original is lost in the translation. Compare the phrases from the free translation with the more literal rendering:

> "Darkness of evening falls" and
> "Blue evening drops";

> "The white light of day dawn
> Yet finds us singing" and
> "The white dawn rises."

In stanzas III and IV, when the phrase *Hitciya yahina-a* stands alone as a line, it has been inserted. It appears in the original, but was omitted by Mr. Russell in his translation. In fact, it concludes every sentence in the song. Observe that the introductory phrase is the same for each stanza. Mr. Russell does not use the full repetition of the original.

75. Lummis, Charles. The Land of Poco Tiempo, pp. 49–50. Scribner's. N. Y. 1902. A corn-grinding song, relating to the birth of the corn.
Line 5. The thunder.
Line 17. The tail of the pheasant.

77. Curtis, Natalie. The Indians' Book, p. 489.

78. Troyer, Carlos. Traditional Songs of the Zuñi Indians. Lines 1 and 2, 8 and 9, 15, 20, and 21 are given as echo calls.

79. *Ibid.*

82. *Ibid.*

83. *Ibid.*

84. Goddard, Pliny Earle. Gotal—a Mescalero Apache Ceremony, Putnam Anniversary Volume, pp. 385–394. This is the fifty-third song, sung at sunrise on the last morning of the ceremony.

85. Matthews, Washington. The Mountain Chant, p. 463. Bur. of Amer. Eth. Washington. 1887.

86. Matthews, Washington. Navaho Myths, Prayers, and Songs, pp. 27–28. University of California Publications, vol. V, no. 2. *Beauty* is synonymous with *happiness* in the Navaho songs.

87. Fletcher, Alice C. The Hako, p. 323.

88. *Ibid.*, p. 324.

89. *Ibid.*, pp. 322–323.

91. *Ibid.*, p. 330.

92. Leland, Charles G. The Algonquin Legends of New England, p. 379.

93. Barbeau, C. M. Huron and Wyandot Mythology, pp. 318–321. Dept. of Mines. Geological Survey, Ottawa, Canada. 1915.

This song-sequence begins with the death of Mah-oh-rah. Seeking to bring her back from the spirit world, her father rides in pursuit across the sky. The Grandmother, guardian deity of the Wyandots, transforms the flying group into stars, Dehn-dek's three stags becoming the stars in the Belt of Orion.

Line 5. The spirit world.

Line 6. *Our Grandmother* was the daughter of the Mighty Ruler of Heaven. The Creation myth relates her accidental fall from heaven, her rescue by the Swans, and the creation of the Great Island (North America) for her home. In her subterranean city, she ruled over the Wyandots with her fiery torch given by the Thunder God. After the Wyandots came out to live on the earth, their spirits visited her on their way to the Land of the Little People.

95. Goddard, Pliny Earle. From the literal translation of Song V, The Masked Dancers of the Apache, Holmes Anniversary Volume, pp. 134–136.

96. *Ibid.*, Song III, p. 134.

97. Russell, Frank. The Pima Indians, p. 280. "On their emergence upon the surface of the earth, the Nether-World people danced together and with Elder Brother sang this song." Since this is an archaic song, with its theme of the beginning of the race, we may consider it, in the original, an example of the earlier rhythms.

98. *Ibid.*, p. 274.

The last four words are added, in Mr. Russell's own words, to show that the original song closes with a repetition of its opening. The complete version, in seventeen lines, uses the opening group three times. This song is archaic; and its rhythm is undoubtedly one of the earlier types.

99. Matthews, Washington. Navaho Myths, Prayers, and Songs, p. 61.

101. Matthews, Washington. The Night Chant, pp. 280–281. Amer. Mus. of Nat. Hist. N. Y. 1902.

102. *Ibid.*, pp. 279–280.

103. Curtis, Natalie. The Indians' Book, pp. 361–362.
104. *Ibid.*, pp. 357–358. Sung to consecrate the hogans, or dwellings, of the gods; and in later times, to consecrate the hogans of the Navahos.
107. *Ibid.*, pp. 363–364.
109. Matthews, Washington. The Night Chant, p. 140.
110. Curtis, Natalie. The Indians' Book, pp. 354–356. Each song is sung four times, with the substitution, in the sixth line, of the name of another mountain.
114. Matthews, Washington. The Night Chant, p. 81.
116. Curtis, Natalie. The Indians' Book, p. 352.
117. Curtis, Natalie. The Indians' Part in the Dedication of the New Museum, pp. 31–32. Art and Archæology, vol. VII.
119. Curtis, Edward S. The North American Indian, vol. I, p. 37. The North American Indian, Inc. N. Y. 1907. *Stenatliha*—woman without parents—goddess of creation.
120. Matthews, Washington. Navaho Legends, pp. 269–275.
    "This prayer is addressed to a mythic thunder-bird. . . .; but the bird is spoken of as a male divinity."
125. Matthews, Washington. Navaho Myths, Prayers, and Songs, pp. 47–48.
    Stanzas II, III, and IV vary chiefly in the first two lines: the conclusion repeats four times, "It is finished in beauty."
128. Matthews, Washington. The Mountain Chant, p. 420.

129. Mindeleff, Cosmos.   Navaho Houses, pp. 504–
    505.   17th Ann. Rep. Part II. Bur. of Amer.
    Eth. Washington. 1898.
131. Curtis, Edward S. The North American Indian,
    vol. III, p. 72.
132. Curtis, Natalie.   The Indians' Book, p. 53.
133. Fletcher, Alice C.   The Hako, pp. 319–320.
135. *Ibid.*, pp. 343–344.
136. Fletcher, Alice C.   The Omaha Tribe, pp. 586–
    587. Bur. of Amer. Eth. Washington. 1907.
138. *Ibid.*, pp. 557–558, p. 573: "In the ritual, the
    primal   rock, . . . that   which   rose   from   the
    waters, is addressed by the term 'venerable
    man.' His assistance is called to the 'little
    ones,' the patients about to be administered to."
142. *Ibid.*, pp. 115–117.
144. *Ibid.*, pp. 119–122.
145. La Flesche, Francis.   The Osage Tribe, pp. 150–
    151.
146. Fletcher, Alice C.   The Omaha Tribe, p. 130. *See
    also* A Study of Omaha Indian Music, p. 39.
    Archæological and Ethnological Papers, Peabody
    Museum, Harvard University. Vol. I, no. 5.
147. The Omaha Tribe, p. 394.
148. Curtis, Natalie.   The Indians' Book, p. 153.
    This Cheyenne song was sung by the old men,
    often from the summit of the hills at dawn.
152. The recessional movement appears in *The Song
    of a Wolf* in Miss Densmore's Teton-Sioux Music,
    p. 190.   Bulletin 61. Bur. of Amer. Eth. Wash-
    ington. 1918.

154. Moulton, Richard G. Literary Introductions: Modern Readers' Bible, pp. 1457–1458.

160–1. Matthews, Washington. (1) The Night Chant, pp. 282–283. (2) Navaho Legends, p. 269.

161. Matthews, Washington. (3) The Night Chant, pp. 294–295.
(4) *Ibid.*, pp. 279–280.

162. Curtis, Natalie. The Indians' Book, p. 10.

163. Cushing, Frank. Zuñi Folk Tales, p. 255.

164. Mr. John P. Harrington is one of the few investigators who have taken account of the use of pitch in an Indian language. His discussion of this element in the Tewa speech may be found in his study of the *Tiwa Language, Dialect of Taos, New Mexico*, page 15. Papers of the School of American Archæology, number 14; also in American Anthropologist, volume 12, number 1. 1910.

166. See Dr. E. W. Scripture's discussion of oral verse, *Die Verskunst und die experimental Phonetik, Wiener Medizenische Wochenschrift*, 1922.

172. *See* Mrs. Mary Austin's The American Rhythm, pp. 3–65.

ACKNOWLEDGMENTS

ACKNOWLEDGMENTS are due to the following persons, societies, and companies for their courteous permission to quote poems on which they hold the copyright:

Austin, Mary:
   The American Rhythm, Harcourt, Brace & Co.; Harper's Magazine.
Barbeau, C. M.:
   Huron and Wyandot Mythology. Dept. of Mines, Geological Survey, Ottawa, Canada.
Burton, Frederick:
   American Primitive Music. Moffat, Yard. Now published by Dodd, Mead.
Converse, Harriet M.:
   Myths and Legends of the New York State Iroquois. New York State Museum.
Corbin, Alice:
   Red Earth. R. F. Seymour, Chicago.
Curtis, Edward S.
   The North American Indian. The North American Indian, Inc., N. Y.
Curtis, Natalie:
   The Indians' Book. Harper's. (Mr. Bridgham Curtis, executor.)
   The Indians' Part in The Dedication of The New Museum, Art and Archæology.

Cushing, Frank:
Zuñi Folk Tales. G. P. Putnam's Sons.
Densmore, Frances:
Chippewa Music. Bureau of American Ethnology.
Dorsey, J. Owen:
The Çegiha Language. Bureau of American Ethnology.
Eastman, Charles A.:
Old Indian Days: McClure. Now published by Little, Brown.
Fletcher, Alice C.:
The Hako; The Omaha Tribe. Bureau of American Ethnology.
A Study of Omaha Indian Music. Peabody Museum, Harvard.
Goddard, Pliny Earle:
Gotal, a Mescalero Apache Ceremony, Putnam Anniversary Volume.
The Masked Dancers of the Apache, Holmes Anniversary Volume.
Myths and Tales of the San Carlos Apache. American Museum of Natural History.
Hale, Horatio:
The Iroquois Book of Rites. Library of Aboriginal Literature, Philadelphia. (Mrs. Daniel Brinton.)
La Flesche, Francis:
The Osage Tribe. Bureau of American Ethnology.
Leland, Charles G.:
Algonquin Legends of New England. Houghton, Mifflin.

Lummis, Charles:
    The Land of Poco Tiempo. Chas. Scribner's Sons.
Matthews, Dr. Washington: Navaho Legends. Hough-
    ton, Mifflin (for Amer. Folk-Lore Society).
    The Mountain Chant. Bur. Amer. Eth.
    The Night Chant. Amer. Mus. Nat. Hist.
    Navaho Myths, Prayers, and Songs. Univ. of
    Cal.
Mindeleff, Cosmos:
    Navaho Houses. Bur. of Amer. Ethnology.
Powell, James:
    Mythology of North American Indians. Bur.
    Amer. Ethnology.
Riggs, A. L.:
    Dakota Songs and Music: Tâh-koo Wah-kán.
    Boston. 1869.
Rink, Henry:
    Tales and Traditions of the Eskimo. Black-
    wood. London. 1875.
Russell, Frank:
    The Pima Indians. Bur. Amer. Eth.
Spinden, Herbert J.
    Home Songs of the Tewa. Amer. Mus. of Nat.
    Hist.
Stevenson, Matilda:
    The Sia. Bur. Amer. Eth.
Troyer, Carlos:
    The Sunrise Call, Hymn to the Sun, Sunset
    Song, Invocation to the Sun God, Lover's Wooing,
    or Blanket Song. From "Traditional Songs of
    the Zuñi." Theodore Presser Co., Philadelphia.

INDEX

[187]

www.ingramcontent.com/pod-product-compliance
Lightning Source LLC
Chambersburg PA
CBHW060644260626
47161CB00008B/2991